Cowboy Heroes of the Southwest

Cowboy Heroes of the Southwest

Published by:
O Slash O LLC.
P.O Box 1
Stanfield, AZ 85127

First Edition

ISBN # 978-0-9853756-0-7 Soft Cover

ISBN # 978-0-9853756-1-4 Hard Cover
ISBN # 978-0-9853756-2-1 E Book

Southwest – Non-fiction

Acknowledgements

A book is a process of many steps. Along the way, many people have a hand in getting the finished product into your hands. I would like to thank, first and foremost, you, the reader, for without a consumer, there is no need for a supplier.

I would next like to thank the wonderful people highlighted herein. Most I know personally, the rest, I feel I do now.

Jo Baeza is a wonderful writer and editor. Upon meeting Jo a few years ago, she inspired me to step up my writing. She took me under her wing and tutored me immensely. I credit her with taking writing to a new level for me. Thanks Jo.

D. Whitcomb has become a friend of mine; divine intervention threw us together, now she has the credit of editing this work. Thank you madam editor.

A-10 Etcheverry is a character and a great artist. He drew the cover picture; thanks A-10. Byron McConnell is a design wizard. He did the cover design, graphics, and also the book design and layout. Thanks Byron.

Thanks also to all my friends and family who have supported me in this crazy transition of becoming a writer. Without your support I would be half as much.

Last, but certainly not least, I credit and thank God. It is only by the grace of God, through His guidance, and talents bestowed upon me, this project has become reality.

Jim Olson

Dedication

This book is dedicated to heroes everywhere, especially my favorite kind – COWBOYS!

Table of Contents

Preface

It seems a bit strange to sit down and write the first part of a book after the rest has already been written, but that's the way it goes. Just like everything else about writing, I learned on the fly. Trial and error you might say. I even started writing by pure accident. It was during the summer of 2005 …

A friend of mine who owned a local magazine came by my office. (I presumed to talk to me about advertising for my ranch sales business.) Instead, he asked me to write an article for his magazine. Astounded, I told him I was not a writer, and besides that, what in the world would I write about? He told me he had a hole to fill in the August issue and that a story on the real estate boom is what he wanted. (He figured me to be an expert on the subject I suppose.)

What he did not know, however, was that I was tired of real estate right about then - because of that very boom going on. I was spending many, many long hours going over contracts, paperwork, etc. I told my friend that very thing, and he left my office promptly with the comment, "Come on, just write me an article."

I thought about it for a while and decided to have a little fun with the deal. A neighbor of mine is the world-famous Dale Smith - famous, that is, in cowboy circles. A lot of folks who live right down the road from Dale have no idea about his lifetime of achievements. So that's what I did. I went and interviewed Dale, took some photos, and gleaned old photos from him as well. I then turned it all in to my friend at the magazine in a sealed manila envelope. I knew he expected an article on the real estate boom to be in there.

I didn't hear a thing for a few weeks and figured the joke I pulled on my editor buddy was either not well received, or it had been forgotten. Then when the magazine came out (August 1, 2005), I started getting calls.

People were congratulating me on such a nice article. They said things like: "I didn't know you wrote." "I never knew all those things about Dale!" "Great job." And on and on ...

Apparently my friend was getting good responses down at the magazine as well, because, a few days later he stopped by my office with a big grin on his face. "Can you do that again?" he asked. "We have had great feedback on your story." I told him I guessed I could, and we made a deal right then and there to start trading my real estate ad each month for an article highlighting a cowboy with an interesting story to tell or who had made a difference in some way or another - positive stories from the country.

Pretty soon another magazine owner I dealt with frequently called and said, "I've been seeing your article in [so-and-so's] magazine. That would work in mine as well. You want to put it in here also?" I told him I did not have time to write two articles per month, but he said the one I already wrote was fine with him as the readership of the two magazines was different. I talked with the first guy about it. He said it didn't bother him, and that is how the monthly "My Cowboy Heroes" column got its start ...I was syndicated! LOL!

From there, the rest is history. I discovered a true love of writing. This book you have in your hands is my third. I often tell the story of how I never aspired to be a writer -it found me. I believe it was meant to be. I have also had a lot to learn along the way about being a writer: Having a knack as a windy storyteller is one thing; being a good writer is completely another. However, I enjoy working daily at honing my craft.

The stories I present to you here in this book are the stories I cut my writing teeth on. This is a collection of articles written over a six-year period. While these articles have appeared in any one of over twenty different publications since I started out, I sincerely hope you will enjoy them as if you are seeing them for the first time. I have gone back, updated, and rewritten the older ones, so it gives the reader a fresh look at all of them.

Go with God, my friend. *Vaya con Dios, amigo.*

Picsindesign.com

What is a Cowboy?
My Opinion

Rodeo cowboy, trail rider, cowboy mounted shooter, feedlot cowboy, cutter, reiner, team roper, barrel racer, ranch hand, horse trainer - what exactly is a cowboy?

According to Webster's, the short answer is, "One who tends cattle and performs many of his duties on horseback." Over 100 years ago, Gene Rhodes simply dubbed him, "The Hired Man A-horseback." However, in modern times, that's not always the case.

Since it began to take hold in the latter part of the nineteenth century, the iconic image of the "Great American Cowboy" has been both idolized and vilified - although most cowboys never asked for either. Many people from around the globe envision cowboys when they think of Americans. While Argentina has its *gauchos* and Mexico its *charros*, being a cowboy is uniquely American. A lot of Americans, however, think of cowboys as anyone who comes from the western part of the United States, wears cowboy-type clothing and listens to country music!

First, let's begin with a little history. The American cowboy originated in the southwestern U.S. He was a spin-off from the *vaqueros* who tended stock there when it was Mexican territory.

After the War Between the States, the country was hungry for beef, and a lot of it was running wild in Texas and other parts of the Southwest. This led to entrepreneurs who dared chase after the "mavericks," as the wild cattle were called. Adapting the trade of the vaquero, these men went into untamed lands in search of large herds of cattle while seeking their fortunes.

The men gathering wild cattle and getting them to market in the East were given credit as being the first American cowboys. We should never forget how these people had a role in taming and settling the wild frontier, making it safe for others to follow.

The occupation was never an easy one. It required a certain type of individual who was long on stamina, independence, and wasn't afraid of hard work or dangerous encounters - encounters that could include a whole assortment of wild creatures besides feral cattle and high-spirited horses. It took a bold type of feller to be a cowboy.

Cowboys were admired for taking great pride in their work. Most possessed a work ethic second to none. Early cowboys were known to be loyal, honest, respectful, hardworking, and independent. They had a clear sense of right and wrong and, perhaps, a streak of wildness. They owed fidelity to their employer, because he entrusted them with an empire. To have the reputation of "top hand," meant you were well respected and could land a job just about anywhere.

Cowboys were expected to do the right thing without being told. If you were shiftless, lazy, or a slacker, your bad reputation usually preceded you. Individuals lacking in desirable qualities were soon run out of the country. (I think they went back East and became politicians.)

As time went on, ranching went from wild trail drives to raising cattle on large places of the West behind barbed wire enclosures. Some consider this the end of the cowboy era. But, as cowboy humorist Baxter Black put it, "There are still plenty of cowboys out there; you just can't see them from the interstate." While civilization marched westward, cowboys evolved and changed with it.

The cowboy image evokes pictures of stalwart men in Stetson hats riding horses in the great outdoors. The first to portray and romanticize this notion were the dime novels, written by predominately Eastern authors, and then sold around the world. Most of the stories were greatly sensationalized in the interest of selling books. Next came moving picture shows (the predecessor of modern-day movies) where cowboy stories were again sensationalized in the interest of sales. As Hollywood and media began to publicize the stereotype of the cowboy, the legend grew.

Your original cowboys were trailblazers of the American West. They generally possessed the character traits discussed earlier, so stories told about them in print and in movies weren't such a far leap. The storytellers were the first, however, to start the ball rolling on what was later to become the cowboy image known worldwide. Guys like Tom Mix, Roy Rogers, and John Wayne; and books by Louis L'Amour and Zane Grey became some of the most recognizable cowboy icons of the twentieth century.

Being a cowboy was not necessarily linked to tending cows anymore; it had a lot to do with how you looked and, more importantly, with how you acted and presented yourself. If you took time to help those in need, if you were of strong moral character, if you were a hard worker, independent, and unwavering in your convictions, you were thought to have cowboy characteristics. What started off as an occupation was transforming into a way of life and a description of character.

Being called a cowboy lumps you in with a large but diverse group of people; different types of cowboys were listed in the beginning of this chapter. It's kind of like a baseball player. To the casual observer, they are all just baseball players. However, a player or avid fan will tell you there are pitchers, catchers, outfielders, infielders, etc. While they all play the same game and represent the same sport, each one is different in what he does.

The same goes for cowboys. The guy living on a ranch fifty miles from the nearest town may be considered a *real* cowboy by some and obviously fits Webster's description. However, if you ask any of those other groups mentioned (i.e. rodeo riders, trainers, mounted shooters, etc.) if they are cowboys, they will also emphatically reply in the affirmative.

I ask the question: Could John Wayne have ridden into the brush on a half-broke horse with a rope and a dog, routed out wild cattle, and then driven them a few miles to a corral? Of course then he would have had to single-handedly brand, load, and haul the critters off to market. Well, I don't like to admit it, but he probably could not have done that. In real life, few people can! Most working cowhands can perform tasks like that quite well. However, you're liable to start a fight if you claim John Wayne was not a cowboy! After all, he presented one of the greatest images of the American cowboy there ever was.

Whether working on the range, or living on an acre with a horse in the backyard, cowboys share some common ground. Generally you will find ranching or agriculture somewhere deep in their roots. More often than not they still have ties to being rural, whether it is through hunting, living in the country, or raising animals. Some wear hats as a fashion statement, others to keep shaded from the sun. Aside from those superficial elements, you can almost always find the desirable characteristics of the original cowhands in them. And they're everywhere in America—north, south, east, and west.

In my younger days, I had the distinct honor of working as a "hired man a-horseback." At the time I thought that unless you were punchin' cows, you could not be considered a cowboy. I realize now it was only youthful ignorance causing me to think that way. Today I have a much broader view of what being a cowboy really is. I've met people in the movie business, construction, selling tires, weekend ropers, rodeo folk, businessmen, as well as many other occupations, all of whom I consider to be cowboys. It's just that tending cattle and performing many of your duties a-horseback has less and less to do with it nowadays.

Now what makes some of them heroes? I reply by saying that just about everyone is a hero to someone. The folks highlighted in this book just happen to be people I've run across or heard about in my travels. Some are well-known; others are unknowns ... but I consider each and every one of them as having a worthwhile story to tell, and I hope you enjoy meeting them as I have.

Don't forget cowboys come in the female version as well. Called cowgirls, you could insert that word for cowboy anywhere in this story and it would still read true. As a matter of fact, some great ones are highlighted in the following chapters.

While insiders may know the difference between a bull rider and a mounted shooter, or a barrel racer and a team penner, the world looks at us all through the same lens. So I conclude by saying, "Persons displaying certain cowboy characteristics and truly promoting the Western way of life should all be considered COWBOY."

Jim Olson

Cundo
From a Wheelchair to Horseback

When you see a young man lifted out of a wheelchair onto a horse, it fills your heart with joy as he rides around … unassisted. When that same man enters the rodeo arena to compete against non-handicapped persons, you stand up and cheer! And when he wins, you attempt to immortalize him in writing.

Secundino Lizarraga Jr. is a cowboy—more specifically, a heeler. Not a "healer" as in a medicine man or doctor, but a "heeler" as in a cowboy who ropes the hind feet of cattle in competition.

Secundino, affectionately known as "Cundo" by friends and family, is not your everyday ordinary ol' heeler; he epitomizes the phrase "Cowboy Up." If you look up the words "try," "cowboy," "tough," or anything along those lines in a dictionary, you're liable to see a picture of Cundo (or, at least, in my opinion, you should). This young man has the heart of a champion, the tenacity of a bulldog and the biceps of a weight lifter.

There are thousands of cowboy heelers across this great land, and some are very good at it, but I'm unable to recall any others confined to a wheelchair and still good - even great - at it.

This young man grew up near Maricopa, Arizona. Like a lot of country kids, he was introduced to riding and roping at an early age. His father competed in Mexican rodeos when he was younger, and, to this day, he still enjoys the occasional roping competition as a participant. It was only natural for Cundo to follow in the family rodeo tradition.

He says he was roping from a horse by the age of ten. Working on honing his skills over the next couple of years, he improved rapidly … then one day, a life-changing event occurred.

In June of 1998, Cundo was twelve. He'd spent a summer day helping out around the ranch. He recalls loading hay and doing chores throughout a hot desert morning. At one point he felt tired and overheated, so he went into the house where it was cool to take a nap. When he awoke, his lower body didn't feel right. He was unable to stand completely upright and struggled to make his way down the hall.

Within a period of about thirty minutes, Cundo had lost all feeling in his lower body except a numbing, burning feeling. His mom immediately took him to the hospital in Casa Grande. From there he was rushed by helicopter to St. Josephs Children's Hospital in Phoenix, where he spent the next month. Doctors finally diagnosed him as having transverse myelitis, a virus that attacks the central nervous system (similar to polio). It was devastating news. Paralysis!

The next couple of years were especially hard on Cundo. Getting used to life in a wheelchair is quite an adjustment for anyone. A teenager dealing with adolescent issues has enough pressure as it is. Then you throw in being newly handicapped, and I'm sure you get the picture. By the age of fifteen, however, he was determined to try riding his beloved horses once again.

At that point, Cundo had undergone a lot of physical therapy, but only had slight feeling in his lower body. Most of the time, he still experienced burning pain. Yet one thing he noticed right away about horseback riding was that it helped get some feeling back in his lower body.

Eventually, he decided to try roping off of a horse again. It was an awkward situation. Not being able to use one's legs for stability and balance proved to be a challenge. But, with time, he got used to using only his upper body. The horse had to get used to it also.

In the beginning, Cundo and his father would only chase after very slow cattle. Before long, he got better at this, but, when asked about it, he admits there was an incident where a steer was going a little faster than normal, and his horse hustled around behind the steer like he thought he was supposed to. Cundo didn't quite make the corner with the horse and wound up on its side, holding onto the saddle with one hand and the horse's mane with the other. Luckily the horse had sense enough to stand still while a couple of guys got Cundo upright once again.

Early on, Cundo experimented with different methods of staying in the saddle, finding that being strapped around the waist with his feet taped or tied into the stirrups worked best. The first method of stability he used was to take a *latigo* strap, tie it to the back D-rings of the saddle, and then buckle it around his waist.

Using this method - and with a lot of practice and dedication - he quickly became a good roper. In fact, he won his first saddle in 2002! There happened to be a man present at that competition who owned a saddle shop. This man had an idea about how to make Cundo's saddle better and asked if he could take it for a couple days. Cundo reluctantly agreed - it being his first new saddle and all.

The modification made was to bolt an old seat belt from a GM truck into the saddle using the holes where *conchos* normally go on the rear skirting. Cundo was very happy with the upgrade and found the seat belt more convenient to use. He uses that same GM seat belt today, even though it presently resides on yet another new trophy saddle.

Cundo's horses are special animals. They are magnificently trained and really take care of their rider. He predominantly rides a beautiful gray gelding named *Galan* (meaning gallant or gentlemanly in Spanish), which he and his father raised and trained themselves. The name fits the horse, as he is a refined-looking specimen.

Cundo had this to say about riding: "Galan works like nobody's business. The horses I ride need to be used to me, because I cannot ride them using my legs like most horses are accustomed to. I can slightly pick up my legs and let them fall back against a horse as if to kick a little bit, but ninety-nine percent of my riding is done with my upper body and by shifting my weight in the saddle."

When queried whether he's ever felt self-pity, anger, or asked, "Why me?" Cundo replied: "At first I was a little bitter, but then I decided the only thing to do was make the best of it. I believe God has a bigger plan for all of us, and I am actually thankful that I'm able to use my condition to inspire people. Some other people may have not taken being in this condition so well ... I can handle it just fine."

He goes on to give advice, not only to others who suffer handicaps, but people in general. "I can do anything that anyone else can do; I just have to try a little harder at some things. Any person can do anything they want if they think of ways to get it done and give it 110 percent."

On almost any given weekend, you can find Cundo at a roping competition somewhere in the Southwest. During one six-month period, he won three trophy saddles, and one year, he claimed eight different championship buckles. He practices regularly and works hard at honing his cowboy skills.

He always wins more than his fair share of cash and prizes. Many cowboys without any sort of handicap would love to have a winning resume like he has, but he doesn't use his handicap as a crutch. Always with a smile on his face, Cundo just tries harder and cowboys up!

Cundo is an inspiration to many. When his name is called at a competition, people flock to the fence to get a better look at this dynamo. People who know him say over and over what a great guy he is. He doesn't want to be treated any different than anybody else. Segundino Lizarraga Jr. possesses the ultimate in *cowboy spirit* and *cowboy try*!

Russell Hill

Rob Krentz

Rancher to Martyr

The secure border issue has gotten more press than a political love scandal. It seems everybody has an opinion on the subject and most are quite vocal. But you know what they say about opinions ...

While this subject isn't new by any stretch of the imagination, if you could point to one thing in recent years bringing it to the forefront of political issues, it would have to be the murder of a Southern Arizona rancher on his own property. On that day, March 28, 2010, Rob Krentz became the poster child for the secure border issue. Unfortunately, it cost him his life.

Rob is, without a doubt, one of the most widely known ranchers in America - maybe the world. Just ask anyone anywhere to name an American rancher today, and he or she will likely say Rob Krentz, or, at least, "You know ... that guy who got killed down along the border," because he has received so much media attention.

As I read with interest the stories concerning the border and immigration, I started to wonder, "Just who was Rob Krentz?" I mean the *person*, Rob Krentz, not the image or martyr he has become for the secure border issue. When one of the Krentz Ranch neighbors approached me about writing on the subject, I readily agreed on the condition it was with the family's blessing, and it would be a story on the man himself, not the political issues. I am honored they agreed, because now I feel as if I know who Rob Krentz really was. I only wish I could have met him prior to that fateful day.

During interviews with family members and neighbors of Rob's, I received glowing reports of a great man: friend, family man, conservationist, good rancher, and kindhearted were all thrown about. Of course, they wouldn't have bad things to say about one of their own, I thought, but you know what? I read articles and contacted several people who are on the other side of the political issue, if you will, and couldn't find one single person who had anything bad to say about Rob. Even those most adamant about immigrant rights had nothing bad to say about Rob Krentz himself; all they wanted to talk about was the issue of the border itself. Here is why:

Rob Krentz was a man of values. From the time he was a little boy, Rob's dad, Bob, drilled into him the importance of doing things the right way. Throughout his life, Rob worked extra hard on doing just that. He wouldn't cut corners when it might have been easy to do so. Little things some people don't think twice about like moving cattle without the proper inspection papers or running red (illegal) diesel in his pickup truck were out of the question as far as Rob was concerned. You never cheat, not even one little bit. Rob lived by those words, and he inspired friends and family in the same way.

To understand Rob, you need to know more about his family history. The Krentz family emigrated from Alsace-Lorraine (which once was a little country between Germany and France and now is part of France) around 1900. They were butchers by trade and first went to St. Louis, Missouri. Family lore says, after government regulations became too cumbersome (even back then) in St. Louis, the Krentz family headed west and settled in Winslow, Arizona, about 1902, operating a butcher shop and a ranch.

While operating the Chevlon Creek Ranch south of Winslow, the family recorded one of the earliest brands in the state of Arizona, the "111 bar" brand. In 1907, the family sought new ventures in the border town of Douglas, Arizona, which was booming at the time. The Krentzes bought the historic Tovrea Meat Market in Douglas and also the Spear E Ranch at the foot of the Chiricahua Mountains. In about 1918, the meat market was sold, and they concentrated efforts solely on ranching from then on.

It took several years, but eventually the family was able to buy up little homesteads surrounding them as they became available. Back then, just about everyone in that country had a section or two of land they had homesteaded. As people went broke or moved away, the Krentz family was in a position to buy the smaller outfits and eventually put together one big ranch. Most of their pastures had been individual homesteads at some time and are named after the original homesteaders. Each has its own history as well.

In circulating media reports, the Krentz ranch is said to be 35,000 acres. Family members say, "That isn't quite right, but it is impolite to ask a person the size of their spread. It's kind of like asking people how much money they have in the bank. Only the IRS and our banker are privy to that information."

The family members were pioneers. They were the kind of people who settled and developed this country and made it safe for others to follow. Today, they are the kind of family considered to be the backbone of America. Surviving bad droughts, cyclical markets, government regulations, and myriads of other issues have made them the strong ranching family they are.

Rob and his dog Blue. Photo provided by Krentz family

The Krentz Ranch has existed since before Arizona was a state. It was there long before the United States Forest Service came along and started dictating rules to them. This is the background and legacy that Rob was born into - a salt-of-the-earth kind of old-time ranching family.

When asked about some of Rob's other qualities, over and over again I am told about his willingness to help out. Rob's wife, Sue, says, "Most of the time when Rob left the house he would say, 'I am going to help ol' so and so.'" Rob's neighbors all have great stories to tell about Rob going out of his way to help them out of a jam. Not only would he help a neighbor, but he was kind to strangers as well, including the illegal immigrants inundating his property.

Rob was known to help out a thirsty, starving, or wounded immigrant on more than one occasion. In fact, that may have been what got him killed. Rob's last radio transmission to his brother, Phil, was something like, "Going to help an illegal in distress." Rob and his dog, Blue, were found shot several hours later.

Friends and family could not stress strongly enough that Rob loved to help people. "A friend in need is a friend indeed" was a motto of Rob's. Not only did he help out friends and strangers in and around the ranching country of southeastern Arizona, but Rob was very involved in many other projects as well.

Rob was active in the cattle grower's associations at the local and state levels. He worked with the Malpai Borderlands group trying to preserve ranching and wildlife habitat for future generations. He testified numerous times to congressional leaders about issues regarding the international border and always seemed to find the time to continue helping out where he could.

The Krentz family is well-known as a good steward of the lands it controls. Family members have been honored for practices such as their long, gravity flow water pipeline serving cattle and wildlife across their expansive ranch. Rob and his family took such good care of their land that they were used as examples of range stewardship on numerous occasions, and, to top it off, the Krentz Ranch was inducted into the Arizona Farming and Ranching Hall of Fame in its inaugural year, 2008.

The good-natured Rob was a favorite at brandings on nearby ranches. He was nicknamed "Crunch" and everybody laughs as they recall the "Krentz crunch" that Rob used on waspy calves. He was a large man physically and, after watching younger or smaller cowhands get mucked out by an unruly yearling, Rob would come running and put the Krentz crunch on the offending animal. Folks laugh when they describe the move as a cross between tackle football, wrestling, and cowboying.

Rob loved to hunt, fish, and do just about anything outdoors. He was a good roper, rancher, horseman, cowman, husband, and father.

"He was easy to get along with."

"He was always positive."

"He was a genuine kind of person."

These are just some of the quotes given about Rob.

Rob would constantly tell his family, "We are very blessed: We are blessed to live in this beautiful place we live in; we are blessed to live the lifestyle we want to and do what we want every day." Rob Krentz was an exemplary human being. As one of Rob's friends put it, "Rob was one of the good guys; he was a good ol' boy."

David Zickl

Rob Krentz (Part II)

A Friend in Need

Ol' Don calls Rob up one day and said, "Hey Rob, I've got this prolapsed cow over at the Double Adobe Ranch locked up in the corral, and I was wondering if you could give me a hand?"

"Sure," says Rob, "just come on over and get me on your way."

So the two men went to the Double Adobe Ranch, about an hour away from Don's main ranch at the wide spot in the road known as Apache, Arizona. They didn't take a horse with them, because Don had caught the cow in the corral earlier. Upon their arrival, they found a mean ol' gal, none too happy about her current uncomfortable condition or the arrival of the two would-be cowboy doctors.

"You run her up the alley, and I will catch her with the head gate," Don instructed.

After giving Rob quite a runaround, he finally got her headed up the lead-up. She was really moving fast as she hit the front of the chute. As a matter of fact, she hit the front with such a force that the old bolts holding the head gate in place just popped like buttons on a shirt!

The cow then proceeded to run around the corral with the head gate on her head and Don still holding on to the lever. He didn't want to let her go for fear she would escape, or worse, chase him around while wearing the gate.

After a minute or so of dragging Don around, the cow smartened up and backed out of the contraption until she was free of it. She then chased Don around until at last she changed plans, clearing the top rail of the fence like a hurdler at a track meet.

Laughing at the sight of all this, Rob said, "Well, now what are we going to do, boss?"

It would take about two hours to go back to the main ranch and get a horse, so Don rummaged around behind the seat of his truck until he came up with an old catch rope.

"We'll rope her using this truck; we don't need a horse," declared Don. "You drive!"

Rob said, "Your ranch … your cow … your truck … you drive. I'll rope!"

So off they went across the mesquite flat, dodging bushes and arroyos, chasing after the prolapsed cow. They tied the rope to the gooseneck ball on the back of the truck. Rob had fashioned a handhold onto the headache rack for balance and support. After chasing the cow far enough, she finally began to wear out and slow down a bit. Don lined her out in a fairly level area, and, when he pulled up beside her, Rob swung a time or two and landed a loop that would have made a professional roper proud.

Rob laid the trip over the right hip, and Don turned the pickup off left, just as if he was in Cheyenne at the Frontier Days! The truck didn't quite work like a good quarter horse would have, so the cow was difficult to throw down. Don figured that, after a while, the old cow would just choke down enough so they could tie her up, and doctor her … but the ole gal was too smart for that. She always kept just enough slack in the rope to keep her breath.

As Don and Rob tried many different methods of getting the cow down, about all they accomplished was to make the cow real mad. Very mad! So mad, as a matter of fact, she spent all of her time trying to chase the two cowboy doctors. Around the truck, in the cab, on the back, it didn't matter; she was after her antagonists with a vengeance.

Finally the two men came up with a plan. They rummaged around behind the seat and found another catch rope. This one they tied to the base of a large mesquite bush nearby.

Don said, "Let her chase you by here, and I'll heel her."

Rob said, "Your cow … your ranch … you chase. I'll rope."

So, as Don let the cow chase him around like a champion bullfighter, he finally got her to go by the spot where Rob patiently waited. With a heel shot sent by the gods, Rob snagged a hind leg. Then Don jumped in the truck and took up the slack; the cow was tied down. Then, and only then, was slack given back into the ropes.

Well, they got her parts put back where they belonged and sowed her up, then cautiously let her go. Both men were worn out from the ordeal. As they headed back toward home, Don told Rob, "I sure do thank you for helping me out pard'. That would have been quite a job for one man."

Rob replied, while wearing a big grin, "Well, that's what friends are for."

This is a true account as told by a neighbor when asked, "Just what kind of friend was Rob Krentz?" We should all be so lucky as to have friends like Rob Krentz.

Jim Olson

Courtesy of Chavez family

Eddie Chavez
From a Pauper to a King

Eddie Chavez was born in 1934 on the family ranch between Springerville and St. Johns, Arizona, in a small rock home. Eddie passed away in 2005, and, at the time of his passing, he lived in a very nice home on the side of South Mountain overlooking the Phoenix valley. Most people would say that Eddie lived very comfortably at the end of his days; some would call him wealthy, and others might say he was rich. Eddie didn't concern himself with stuff like that.

What lies in between those years of 1934–2005 are what makes telling a bit about Eddie Chavez's life a worthwhile story. I call it, the classic tale of the American dream.

The Chavez family has been ranching in the northeastern part of Arizona near Lyman Lake for several generations. Although most historians claim the Mormon settlers were the first non-Indians to settle that part of the world, the Chavez family claims to have been there longer. As proof, they offer up an old gravesite on the family ranch with a headstone dating back to the early part of the 1800s, a good fifty or sixty years before any other settlers arrived. "Our ancestors were ranching and farming in this valley long before any other white people came," says family historian and Eddie's youngest daughter, Antoinette, "and we are still here today." It was into this deep-rooted, old-time family that Eddie was born.

About that same time, a young girl named Victoria Gabaldon was born on another historic family ranch at Mangas, New Mexico. Victoria and her family moved from the family ranch to Springerville, Arizona while she was still a teenager. As fate arranged, young Eddie Chavez and Victoria Gabaldon met at a football game in Springerville; each was fourteen at the time. By the age of eighteen, they were married. Together through thick and thin from then on, they only parted upon Eddie's death. Even then, his spirit still lives on in Victoria - and many other family members as well.

As a young married couple, they set out for Phoenix, where Eddie was to work in construction. Like most young married folks, they had big plans and dreams. Eddie and Victoria were no strangers to hard work, and hard work is what they got plenty of for a long time. Eddie sometimes worked up to three different jobs while Victoria took care of the kids, which came to number five of their own, while adding two more belonging to other relatives along the way.

Together they also built their home with their own hands near the Laveen area southwest of Phoenix. On most weekends, the Chavez family would head back up the mountain to the family ranch and work there as well. Those first several years were quite a struggle, but the young family kept a good attitude and always maintained a good work ethic. With Eddie working for the state highway department and various other construction jobs, and Victoria taking care of the kids and helping Eddie with the house construction, the young family eked out a living. Then tragedy struck.

Eddie and Victoria lost their only son in a car accident when he was still a teenager. It was a devastating loss for the two of them, as one can only imagine. However, out of this tragedy, a good thing did come about. As a way to keep Victoria's mind off of her tragic loss, the family opened its own business and started selling Mexican food. They worked out of a little stand at the South Fork Ranch near Springerville that summer, selling food to the tourists. Eddie worked on the place, getting it ready for customers, while Victoria cooked in the kitchen.

Now, Victoria is an excellent cook—and I do mean *excellent*. She learned to cook from her family and had been cooking for large numbers of people ever since she was a little girl. Not only is Victoria a great cook, but the food she cooks is that old-time "Rio Grande"–style food, which her family had been cooking ever since migrating up the Rio Grande Valley of New Mexico several generations back. The Arizona tourists loved it, and soon her great cuisine would be known worldwide.

That first summer at South Fork Ranch went so well that the next year Eddie and Victoria decided to open a restaurant in Springerville. Eddie built a little A-frame building on Victoria's parents' land in town with fairly good visibility. From that humble beginning, the famed Los Dos Molinos restaurants sprang. Now there are five different Los Dos Molinos locations, including four in the Phoenix area and, of course, the original in Springerville. The Springerville restaurant was later rebuilt (by Eddie's own hands) at a new location on Highway 60. Yet, becoming successful restaurateurs didn't happen overnight.

People loved Victoria's food, and Eddie was handy with making the place look good and keeping things working, but money was still tight. From that modest little A-frame beginning to the legend that they are today took a lot of struggle and hard work. Eddie and Victoria didn't

House Eddie lived in when he died. *Photo by Jim Olson*

have any financial backers. They didn't have the support of a national franchise or a big-time banker to catapult them to profitability. They relied on their own hands and the support of their large family. You might say that they built their legacy one plate of delicious food at a time, one satisfied customer at a time.

After the restaurant in Springerville took off and started doing well, the couple opened one in Mesa. It was kind of the same scenario: Eddie had to work hard on the place to get it going while Victoria did all of the cooking. The restaurant on South Central in Phoenix came next. It was an old-time hacienda that had been badly vandalized over the years. There was a lot of history there however, and Victoria wanted a restaurant in that location very much. Once again the couple took over the task of building (or in this case, rebuilding) their restaurant from the ground up.

This little scenario worked well for the Chavez family. Their kids helped out as well. One daughter even opened a restaurant in New York City for several years. Other locations were added near central Phoenix and Chandler. The Chavez family and their chain of Los Dos Molinos restaurants were doing well. People from all over the world and from all walks of life just couldn't get enough of Victoria's great New Mexico-style food! Their slogan soon became "Some like it hot!" as Victoria didn't know how to make it any other way. But along the way, tragedy struck again.

Another of Eddie and Victoria's kids was killed in a car accident. This time it was a daughter, who left behind a now motherless granddaughter. Eddie and Victoria finished raising their granddaughter as if she was their own daughter. The Chavez family had to endure a lot of pain and hardship throughout their lives, but they always pressed on and overcame it.

Throughout the years, Eddie remained passionate about and directly connected to the family ranch. Back when they were first starting out, they raised chickens, sheep, goats, pigs, and even had a milk cow just so they could survive. They grew as much of their own food as possible because money was tight. But even later on in life, when Eddie could afford just about anything that he wanted, he still raised animals. He was a natural born stockman at heart.

House where Eddie was born near St. Johns.   *Photo by Jim Olson*

Eddie also thoroughly enjoyed fixing old things up. He loved the history behind antique items. At the time of his death, Eddie had quite a collection of antique cars that he had remodeled. Then, of course, there is the famous South Central restaurant location, which is a great remodeling of an old-time hacienda building. Both the Chavez and Gabaldon families have a lot of ranching history along the Arizona/New Mexico border area, and Eddie was always picking up old family heirlooms and restoring them.

As a matter of fact, that is how the Los Dos Molinos restaurants got their name. One day when Eddie and Victoria were working on their original little place before it was open, they asked each other, "Well, what are we going to call our new restaurant?" There just happened to be a couple of old chili grinders sitting there that Eddie had brought out for decoration. One was from his old family ranch and the other from hers. They looked at each other, then at the old family grinders or *molinos* as they are called in Spanish - they knew right then they had their answer. Thus the Los Dos Molinos (or The Two Grinders) name came about. Victoria says they were always "grinding it out" anyway!

Eddie was a very good-natured fellow. He was constantly kidding and joking. I guess that having a good attitude helps to overcome the trials and tribulations of such hardships as they endured. Through all of the financial slow times, tragedies, and other struggles, Eddie and Victoria kept positive attitudes. They were the same good-natured and down-to-earth people later in life heading the Los Dos Molinos restaurants' legend as they were when born on those little old remote ranches in the high country rangelands.

Eddie and his family were dealt tragedies, but kept on fighting, always looking upward and onward. Throughout his life, Eddie was a hard-working country kid who never forgot his roots. In the end, he was proud of the legacy left for his family.

Eddie Chavez is a classic example of someone who set out in search of the American dream and had it come true. Born a pauper on a desolate little ranch in northeastern Arizona and died a king on the hillside overlooking the Phoenix valley … that was Eddie Chavez.

Jim Olson

Fred and Deborah Fellows

Cowboy Artists

A large metal sign bearing the brand "backward F, forward F" welcomes you to a ranch outside of Sonoita, Arizona. It is a beautiful place, reminding you more of upper central California or the Davis Mountain country northeast of Marfa, Texas. With its large oak trees and rolling grassland hills at an elevation of around 5,000 feet, it is definitely one of the more beautiful spots in the Southwest. It is the home of many fine ranches, cowboys, and cowgirls.

She was inducted into the National Cowgirl Hall of Fame (the second lady from Arizona after Sandra Day O'Connor). She is a lifetime member of the National Sculpture Society. Her monumental sculptures appear in about two-dozen locations across the country, including the Hall of Champions in Colorado Springs, Colorado; the Horseshoe and South Point casinos in Las Vegas; several Boy Scout of America monuments; several Vietnam Veteran War Hero monuments; and numerous museums. The full list is long and impressive. Her name is Deborah Copenhaver Fellows (Deb to those who know her).

He is the longest living member of the Cowboy Artists of America (CAA). He has served three different terms as the CAA president and, at the time of this writing, is the current director. His art adorns places like the Buffalo Bill Cody Museum in Cody, Wyoming; the Phoenix Art Museum in Phoenix, Arizona; and the Desert Caballeros Museum in Wickenburg, Arizona. His art has graced the cover of over two-dozen magazines and has earned honorable mentions in articles in dozens more. A work of his entitled "We Pointed Them North" has become the logo for the Cowboy Artists of America and the Traditional Cowboy Arts Association's annual sale and exhibition held at the National Cowboy & Western Heritage Museum. His name is Fred Fellows.

Many great accomplishments of these two famous artists are well documented. A simple Internet search will turn up a multitude of information on the art of this talented duo. When you visit with them, however, they prefer to tell you about team roping, ranching, and raising horses. They are quick to point out that their art is, "... art from experience." Drawing and sculpting what they know and love, it is their passion.

First and foremost, they are true Westerners. Fred is a lifelong team roper (header) with an eye for a good head horse. Deb is the heeler of the team, and she has a family rodeo history, which includes her dad (Deb Copenhaver) and brother (Jeff Copenhaver), both world champion cowboys in their respective generations. The Fellows family has competed in rodeo events most of their lives.

Deb, once Miss Rodeo Washington and a runner-up to Miss Rodeo America, looks like you would expect a former rodeo queen to look

Fred explains real-life props he uses. *Photo by Jim Olson*

Deb talks about making a sculpture. Photo by Jim Olson

like. However, upon closer inspection, you see a gal tough as any man, sporting a much nicer exterior. Roping, cowboying and many long hours with sculpturing tools have made her as tough as her male counterparts. Pretty and proper to look at, yet tough as nails, she is quite an impressive woman.

Fred is the quintessential cowboy. Rugged good looks on a six-foot-plus frame with a large cowboy hat leave no question that this is a guy who has spent much time outdoors on the back of a horse.

Fred likes to talk roping horses and is quick to mention a horse he once owned that was a brother to the great horse, Walt, owned by professional roper, Travis Tryan. A mutual friend in Montana, Walt Vermendahl, raised both horses. One day Fred decided that his horse was not being put to its full potential, being turned out in a pasture on the Fellows ranch, so he wound up selling him. The horse then ended up where its brother once was, in the Tryan rope herd. The horse has been a winner at the professional level since.

Fred is an avid history buff on just about anything cowboy or Indian. His collection of Old West memorabilia is one of the most extensive private collections you will find anywhere. He knows the history of each and every piece, how it was used, and where it came from. This knowledge comes in handy when working on art. If one of them is working on a piece depicting the 1800s, early 1900s, or contemporary times, they pay attention to minute details, such as getting the clothing, tack, and accessories correct for the period. Deb says, "In my opinion, it takes away from a piece if it's supposed to be late 1800s, and the horse is wearing a hackamore that wasn't even invented until the 1940s."

Deborah also has a passion for good running horses. At the time of this writing, the couple has 14 head of horses on their ranch near Sonoita. Each has a roping horse or two; everything else is racehorse stock. The ones who don't pan out on the track are then used as barrel racing and rope horse prospects. Deb is passionate about the bloodlines of the horses and laughs as she says, "I often trade stud fees for art ... That comment has gotten me more than one strange look at formal gatherings, but eventually I explain what paying stud fees means to someone in the horse business." Some of their more notable horses are Corona Cartel, Streaking La Jolla, and Treis Seis, all of which have had their share of success on the track.

The couple mentions the fact they have been on and worked with some of the West's most famous ranches. This is an important factor, which carries over to their artwork. The Parker ranch in Hawaii; Haythorn Ranch in Nebraska; the Padlock and I X ranches in Montana; the JA, 6666 and o6 ranches in Texas; and the Y7 ranch of New Mexico are but a few of the ranches they have been around.

After twenty-one-plus years of marriage, the two still act more like newlyweds than a couple approaching the milestone "silver" anniversary. They spend each day working side by side in their luxurious art studio on the ranch. Fred says, "A typical day is to go out to the studio after breakfast, and we each work on our respective projects. After lunch together, we go back out and work till late afternoon. Then we might saddle up some horses and run a few steers, coming back in the evening to go over our projects together. It is much better to have two sets of eyes critiquing our work than one. Sometimes I will see little things Deb has overlooked and visa-versa." The two spend most of their time together, truly enjoying each other's company.

Whether traveling the West, gaining experience on some of its famous ranches, or working with their own animals at home, Fred and Deborah Fellows take pride in transferring the real West into their highly acclaimed artwork.

Here we have a couple that have proven that following your passion in life pays off. They not only do what they love, it has been a lifelong study in search of perfection. Be the best you can at doing what you love - the rest will fall into place.

Jim Olson

Susan Cooper

Don Kimble

Rancher & Rodeo Man

When doing an Internet search of "Don Kimble," you'll find several links to interviews and quotes regarding the secure border issue of Southeastern Arizona. He is an authority on the subject, and people far and wide have asked his opinion. Long before he became famous for that, however, Don was a well-known rodeo cowboy, and, before that, he was known as a top ranch hand.

In the 1950s, Don attended school at a one-room schoolhouse in Apache, Arizona. He now has been a member of that school board since 1984. Today, much the same as it's always been, the one-room school is a place for the local ranch kids of the San Bernardino and San Simon valleys to start their education. At the time of this writing, there are nine kids (grades one thru eight), a teacher, teacher's aide, and three school board members making up the entire faculty, administration, student body, and board.

You might say Apache, located forty miles northeast of Douglas, is little more than a wide spot in the road. There are a few dozen widely scattered ranches and about as many families to match in this secluded, remote area along the New Mexico-Arizona line.

However, an interesting side note from the area is that there are numerous National Finals Rodeo (NFR) qualifications credited to the folks calling this ranch country home. Kimble, Darnell, Glenn, and Snure are some of the names that, not only ranch here, but also have competed at "the Show."

This is the story of Don Kimble; a man who qualified for the NFR while holding down a full-time teaching job and was a college rodeo coach and rancher - all at the same time!

The Kimble family migrated to Arizona around 1919 from Oklahoma and Texas. The women of the family claim it was because of the good ranching country. The men joke the other reason is because Prohibition was in effect and Agua Prieta, Mexico (just across the border), had whiskey available in large quantities ... and it was legal.

Today, Don Kimble lives in the house he was born in on the ranch. He is the third generation of Kimbles to ranch there. The remote, scenic place straddles the New Mexico-Arizona state line between Lordsburg, New Mexico, and Douglas, Arizona. He's proud of this heritage and points out that one of his great uncles died at the Alamo while the family was still in Texas. As a matter of fact, Kimble County, Texas, is named for that uncle.

As a kid, Don learned the art of ranching from his grandfather and father. He learned to ride, rope, and doctor cattle for screwworms after branding season. He says they used to ride all day roping and doctoring those screwworm cattle. "I was probably twelve when I started roping range cattle."

About then is when Don also became his own cattleman. "I started building my herd of cattle when I was twelve, running them on the family ranch. By the time I went to college, my herd had grown enough that I leased a ranch of my own. I've been in the cattle business my whole life."

Don attended high school in Douglas and then went to Cochise Community College (also in Douglas) for two years before completing his education at the University of Arizona, Tucson. While in college, he maintained good enough grades to be listed in "Who's Who among Students in American Universities and Colleges."

Don, by then an avid roper, won the West Coast region of intercollegiate rodeo in the team-roping event all four years he attended college. He competed as both a header and heeler, also entering the bull dogging and calf roping events as well.

After graduating with bachelor of science degrees in animal science and agricultural education, Don worked around Tucson for a couple of years, organizing ropings and doing construction work. Then he became very ill with valley fever, losing a lung as a result. He moved back to Douglas after the ordeal, taking a job teaching agriculture and as the rodeo coach at Cochise Community College. Don was a busy man between running his cattle operation and taking care of his duties at the college, but that didn't stop him from following his roping passion on the side.

In the 1970s, Don was a tough competitor on the Turquoise Circuit of Professional Rodeo, winning the circuit a couple of times. In 1978, he narrowly missed qualifying for the NFR after only going to about fifty rodeos in his spare time. So, in '79, he set a goal of getting there. While still holding down a full-time position at Cochise College and managing his own ranching operation, Don qualified for the NFR in the team-roping event as planned. He did this going to only about sixty rodeos throughout the year, while most of the other top fifteen qualifiers went to closer to a hundred rodeos. Don repeated this amazing feat in 1980.

An interesting thing about the '79 and '80 seasons most rodeo competitors wouldn't be able to do is this: Since Don had a teaching job and income from his ranch, he decided that he would put all major checks he won roping into savings. He cashed smaller checks, living, and rodeoing on that and his other income. At the end of the season, he had managed to put away $50,000 (quite a lot of money back then)! He has left that account alone through the present, still having the "rodeo" money stashed away ... just in case.

Other highlights for Don from 1979 include winning in Denver, which was the biggest single rodeo check in team-roping history at that time. He and partner, Kent Winterton, were on the front page of the *Pro Rodeo Sports News* for that. At the NFR in '79, the team won or placed in each of the first five rounds (a pretty amazing feat considering the competition), and they finished fifth in the world as a team.

A rodeo story, which is laughed about in certain circles to this day involves the Fourth of July run one summer. Don, partner Kent, Doyle Gellerman, and Walt Woodard threw in together and chartered an airplane to make as many rodeos as possible during "Cowboy Christmas." One morning, the two teams roped at Prescott, Arizona, then were to go on to West Jordan, Utah, that night then back to Prescott the following day for their second steer. Kent invited his wife and three small daughters along for the turnaround trip as they had family in West Jordan and there was room in the plane. Immediately after take-off, Walt kicked off his boots, reclining for the trip. Next to him sat one of Kent's little girls, who began to get airsick. Not long after, the little girl couldn't handle it any longer and vomited in the most convenient place she could find, which happened to be Walt's boots, sitting on the floor next to her.

While Don, Kent, and Doyle were laughing so hard their sides hurt, Walt kept repeating in disbelief, "She puked in my boots!" It was all in good fun.

After two NFR qualifications, Don settled down to roping mostly at the Turquoise Circuit events and the larger pro rodeos, which he could get to. He remained a tough competitor at the circuit level for years to come.

Summertime was a favorite of Don's, as he could get away from his job and go to prestigious rodeos such as his all-time favorite in Salinas, California. While he's never won Salinas, Don says he always roped well there and managed to pull several large checks from the rodeo.

Don's only regret rodeoing is that he had a chance to head at the NFR, while back in college, for a heeling partner of his who had made the finals. (Remember, then the top fifteen team ropers, regardless of heading or heeling status, made the finals and invited their partners if said partner wasn't also in the top fifteen.) He wound up declining the offer to rope at the finals because he was worried about his grades suffering with missing two weeks of school.

"Looking back now, I wish I would have accepted the invitation and roped. I believe I could've kept my grades up, and then I'd join the elite group of team ropers who have roped at the NFR both as a header and a heeler," says Don.

In 1988, Don's dad, Ralph, became sick with cancer, so Don took over duties at the family ranch, quit teaching college, and slowed down on the rodeo trail. The last professional rodeo he entered was Salinas in 1995. Since then, he has remained a tough jackpot roper and Professional Rodeo Cowboys Association (PRCA) gold card member, placing regularly through the present.

Don's father died in 1991, and he has been a full-time rancher since. It took a couple of years, but Don bought his uncle's portion of the ranch and at present is the majority owner of the original Kimble ranch along with his mother as a partner. He has owned or leased several ranches throughout the years, but his main operation is now centered on the old home place, which, as I mentioned before, has been continuously ranched by his family since 1919 and the days of Pancho Villa.

While Villa raided along the border region back then, the ranchers felt little or no real fear of the Mexican bandit (or revolutionary depending on how you look at him). Today, however, bandits are a real issue in the border areas of Southern Arizona and New Mexico. One of Don's closest friends, Rob Krentz, was murdered on his own ranch in March 2010, and the killing has been linked to the border issues of the area. Don says this is one of the toughest problems facing his part of the country today. Other struggles include the economy and the rising cost of overhead compared to lower returns from cattle sales.

At the Kimble ranch, they leave their bulls out yearlong in the fairly mild climate. As a result, there is always work to do and calves

Don heeling at Oklahoma City. *Photo by Brenda Allen*

to brand. The ranch usually ships about 400 calves both spring and fall. They raise predominately Black Angus- type cattle. The ranch's headquarters sit above the San Bernardino Valley near the entrance to Skeleton Canyon. The scenery is breathtaking. The ranch home was built in 1890, and was originally part of the historic San Simon Cattle Company. Before that, Cochise and Geronimo roamed these lands.

Although he has no kids of his own, Don is respected for his positive work with youngsters. College professor, school board member, father figure to countless young folk, mentor, and friend; he gives over and above where the young are concerned.

Good rancher, good cowhand, roper, a man of his word - all phrases used in describing Don Kimble. A friend of Don's summed it up this way, "Don is a man of his word, a man of integrity, a man of complete trust, and this is something I really admire about him."

Denny Coffin

Gene Aguirre
100 Years of History

The oldest man I have ever known, Don Yginio F. Aguirre, a walking, talking, history book, passed to the next realm March 26, 2011, at the ripe ol' age of 101. Born September 10, 1909, in what was then the Arizona Territory (Arizona became a state in 1912), Yginio (Gene) Aguirre started life on a large, desert, cattle ranch near Red Rock, Arizona.

As a young boy, Gene intently listened to stories told by his dad and uncles - stories of family history told to them by their dads and uncles. These tales were about freighting on the old Santa Fe Trail; fighting wild Indians before the West was settled; developing mines, ranches and businesses; and developing the West in general. These were first and second-hand accounts of the way things actually were in the mid and late 1800s - not stuff merely read in books. These were the stories and traditions young Gene grew up on.

The Aguirre families were Spanish noblemen from the "Old Country" (Spain) before they migrated to "New Spain" (Old Mexico) in the late 1600s and early 1700s. The Aguirres played a part in the settlement of Mexico and soon were among the leading families in Chihuahua and the state of Sonora. By the mid-1800s, however, political ties were strained in Mexico when Don Pedro Aguirre (Gene's great-great-grandfather) backed the wrong politician who wound up losing an election. Then, for "health reasons" (fear of being shot), the family patriarch decided to move his clan northward. The adventurous Aguirres were off to conquer new frontiers in what is now the southwestern United States.

"My Aguirre ancestors were some of the first freighters to haul hundreds of tons of freight across the Santa Fe Trail from Missouri to New Mexico and points beyond," Gene would say, "and the Aguirre family had some of the first, and finest I might add, ranches in the American Southwest. The pioneering Aguirre family helped settle and develop this country through mining, freighting, trading, and ranching during the 1800s, just as they had done in Mexico during the 1700s. You can read the history books and find that many historians have documented the adventures of my family extensively."

When Gene was a boy in the early 1900s, stories told to him had only happened a few years earlier. The details were being recounted to him while still fresh in recent memory. One such story Gene liked to tell is of the time his great-uncle, Epifanio Aguirre, made headlines by being credited with saving the stage that ran from Santa Fe, New Mexico, to El Paso, Texas, back in 1864.

"Uncle Epifanio was traveling with his wife, their two small children, and a couple of servants in a big four-wheeled ambulance with a saddle horse tied behind. They were following the stage and about eight soldiers with wagons brought up the rear. Out in the middle of the *Jornada del Muerto* between Las Cruces and Socorro, they were jumped by a large band of Apaches. They said it was Cochise.

"Luckily only a few of the Apaches were armed with rifles, and the rest just had bows and arrows. When they were attacked, Uncle Epifanio mounted the saddle horse and ran out in front of the stage with a pistol in each hand and the bridle reins in his teeth. He would empty his pistols and clear a path for the stage and then ride back to his coach where his wife would hand him two more loaded pistols. This went on for a while, and it was very touch and go as they tried to lose the Apaches.

"The passengers on the stage and the soldiers also fired at will, but it was said that Uncle Epifanio showed courage above and beyond what any of them had ever seen before. After several miles of a running battle, a small village came into view. It was only then the Apaches finally decided to quit the attack," said Gene Aguirre, some 145 years after the battle.

Years later, south of Sasabe, Arizona, Indians killed Epifanio near the Mexican border. Gene would chuckle slightly and reflect, "Those Indians and my uncle always had a thing for each other."

It is fortunate stories such as this were told to Gene, because he guarded the stories and traditions passed on to him well. Telling other people true history as it was told to him was a favorite pastime of Gene's. Fortunately he did not waste the gift. He wrote four books on the subject of settling the West, Southwestern history, and how his family was involved. Anyone who loves history and Old West tales should have one of his books.

Not only did Gene have a tremendous lineage of pioneers and nobility to his credit, he was a great trailblazer and an accomplished man himself. He grew up living the cowboy's dream on his father's and uncle's ranches in the Red Rock area. These large ranches ran as many as eight to ten thousand head of cattle in their heyday, and the young man had the good fortune to grow up working with some of the best cowboys in the entire Southwest. These cowboys were actually *vaqueros* and had been practicing the art of handling cattle for generations. Most of our current knowledge and traditions of cowboying are direct spin-offs of what old-time vaqueros taught the first Anglo cattlemen back then.

According to Gene, he grew up, "... learning the art of cowboying from the best vaqueros in the land and learning the business of being a cattleman from my family." One of Gene's other great-uncles, Pedro Aguirre, is credited with developing the famed Buenos Aires ranch along the Arizona-Mexico border. This ranch started as a stage stop in the 1860s, went on to run around 15,000 head of sheep and cattle during Pedro's tenure, and now is a large wildlife preserve.

It is only natural that as Gene became his own man, he was destined to follow the ranching traditions of his ancestors. In his early years, Gene ran cattle in northern Mexico and Southern Arizona. He bought, sold, traded, and raised livestock while continuing to help the Aguirre family operations near Red Rock. He kept on ranching and buying cattle in Mexico to be fattened out and sold in America right up until the late 1940s. Then he had a life-changing event happen, and he moved to Old Mexico for a few years.

In the late '40s the dreaded hoof and mouth disease was discovered in Mexico. The United States and Mexican governments decided to fight it there before it spread all across Mexico and inevitably into the United States. Young men from the southwestern United States, who could speak Spanish and had a ranching background, were highly recruited for this mission. So Gene loaded up his young family and moved to Mexico to work on the eradication of hoof and mouth disease or *La Comision Mexico-Americana para la eradicacion de la Fiebre Aftosa* as it was called down there.

During the late '40s and early '50s, Gene worked for the American government on the *Aftosa Comision*. He worked as a livestock inspector, a supervisor of livestock inspectors, and an appraiser of livestock. His tales of those years are comparable to stories of the American frontier from the late 1800s. Imagine a foreigner coming in and telling a poor *campesino* that he is going to shoot all the man's animals, his only means of a living, and then promising the government will make it right with him later. Resistance from the locals was inevitable, but that was part of the task Americans took on. Gene lived and saw a way of life most Americans will never see. Needless to say, he had many adventures.

Gene says, "I saw things that you would not believe today. I forded swollen rivers during flood season on a mule; crossed high mountain passes where the trails were narrow, slippery, and treacherous; and even faced down armed men while standing up for my job ... what was right. It was pretty tricky down there a time or two; it was more like the 1800s than the 1940s."

The accounts of men who went to Mexico during those years are amazing ... downright impressive! Kind of like Old West adventures happening in modern times. The work accomplished in Mexico saved the American cattle industry millions of dollars and tons of headaches. The industry itself wouldn't look the same today if it weren't for those brave men.

While in Mexico, Gene continued his ranching ventures. Every once in a while he would take time off to buy or sell cattle somewhere in Mexico. Even though he had a job, it didn't stop him from running cattle on the side. He leased ranches here and there, or at times put together loads of cattle to be shipped other places. Ranching was in the Aguirre blood.

Drawing of a young Gene Aguirre. Provided by family

When Gene left Mexico upon the completion of the eradication, he came back to Red Rock where he helped run the family operations once again. He also ranched on his own. He felt like he was back where he belonged at the Aguirre family ranches. It was the perfect place for Gene to raise his family.

As Gene got older, he felt more and more that his background and family history were something special. Not only were both special to him and his immediate family, but to the people of the Southwest as well. By the time he reached retirement age, there weren't many people still alive who had firsthand experience with the old-time vaqueros or with pioneering families who had tamed the West. The old stories handed down to him as a boy were now considered historical. People who keep track of history took note.

"In 1976, Arizona, to honor the [American] bicentennial celebration, decided to re-enact the second march of the Don Juan Bautista De Anza expedition, and they chose me to portray the part of De Anza," Gene recalled with pride. Who else should they choose to play the part of a Spanish nobleman and frontiersman but a descendent of the very same?

It was an honor for Gene to be involved in this celebration of the West, especially since his ancestors were involved with the wild frontier. The ride started off in Sonora, Mexico, and wound up in San Francisco, California. Gene participated in the part from Sonora to Yuma, Arizona. In addition, the Historical Society relied heavily upon Gene's knowledge to add authenticity to the event.

"They [the Historical Society] were always asking me about the old *presidial* soldiers my family told me about as a boy," Gene said about preparation for the re-enactment.

After Gene's retirement in the mid-1970s, he became deeply involved with the Arizona Historical Society. Not long thereafter, Gene decided to start writing down what he knew. At times Gene would remember an event about a certain vaquero and himself chasing a wild steer or perhaps gathering wild mustangs, and he would jot it down. He also wrote quite a bit about his experiences in Mexico while on the *Aftosa Comision*. His stories were well-written and entertaining. As a bonus, they are as close as one can get, in modern times, to being first-hand experiences.

Gene researched his family's history all the way back to the Old World in Spain for one of his books. His father and uncles told him stories as a young man, but he took it a step farther and went back to find the documentation.

"I went to ancient churches and government offices all over Mexico and Spain. I poured over all of the old records that I could find. Each place, each new discovery, would lead me to a new adventure in another town," Gene once said of his research. This was quite an undertaking, but well worth it; he was proud of his ancestry.

When asked about the secret of longevity; Gene had this to say, "... Most of all you have to enjoy life. You can't go around worried and stressed out all of the time; you have to have fun. You need to smile." That advice worked well for Gene as he certainly enjoyed a long, full life - over 101 years' worth! Yginio F. Aguirre was a true gentleman, cowboy, and pioneer. Simply put, he was "*un caballero*."

Valerie Juster

Bill Clark

Cowboy Entrepreneur

Bill was a millionaire back when it meant much more than it does today. He used to say, not in a bragging way, but in an encouraging way, "I reached my goal of becoming a millionaire when I was thirty-seven." No small feat, as the date would have been 1961. However, he did not stop there.

Bill's uncle, Fred, used to tell him, "Think big and leave the pack behind." Bill never forgot those words and repeated them often. He used to say Uncle Fred always went for it in a big way. Broke, bankrupt, and riches were cycles that Fred knew about, but, in the end, it was mostly riches. "It's just as easy to go broke over a thousand dollars as it is over a million," Fred would advise, "but the plan is to learn from your mistakes and not go broke at all."

Bill Edward Clark was born near Larned, Kansas, in 1924. At the beginning of the Great Depression, the family headed west to the Galiuro Mountains of Arizona. Bill's parents were schoolteachers, and his mother had landed a job there in a small one-room schoolhouse at a place whose name has long since been erased from maps. He was the only Anglo student at the school where ranchers' and miners' children came to learn. Being the teacher's kid didn't make matters any better. Bill would grin and shrug his shoulders when remembering those early school days, "It made me tough. I learned Spanish, and some Indian words as well ... and to fight."

After a few years, the family relocated to Scottsdale, Arizona, where both parents got better jobs. Bill played football for the (then) six-man Scottsdale High team and graduated in 1942. After high school, he entered the University of Arizona, but soon decided he would rather join the Navy instead, spending World War II on a battleship in the North Pacific. Upon his return to civilian life, Bill embarked upon the trail of a true entrepreneur.

Never one to shy away from hard physical labor, Bill, later in life, was often referred to as "the Energizer Bunny," because he just kept going and going. After the Navy, he went to work for a farmer picking fruit. Instead of taking his paycheck in cash, Bill soon learned he could make a better deal if he took most of it in trade. This was the beginning of his first fruit stand. In true entrepreneur fashion, Bill soon had deals made with several area farmers and had to hire helpers to assist him in his burgeoning business.

Once the fruit stand was going well, Bill expanded into the roofing business. As a roofer, it wasn't uncommon to see him on top of a house in 100-plus-degree heat doing the work himself. Bill, always looking for opportunity, discovered there wasn't much competition in the booming mining area around Globe, Arizona, so he went there. Upon finding the locals a tight-knit bunch, he walked to every house along the main road and offered to do their roof or put new siding on their house for the ridiculously low price of just about what it cost him - with the condition that no one tell the price.

Bill soon had all the advertising he needed as everyone wanted their house to look as good as the ones along the main road, and he bragged that, at one time or another, his crews roofed or sided almost every house in the Globe-Miami area.

Back at the fruit stand (which was in the country at 48th Street and Thomas in Scottsdale), Bill's business had grown to the point where he bought a farm of his own to help keep up with demand. He also opened another fruit stand in the Phoenix area.

As Bill's enterprises grew, he expanded the farming operation as much as possible. (Farming and ranching were close to his heart.) Before long he had his own packing company (Clark Packers of Tempe) and owned a big part of the citrus-growing land around what is today

Queen Creek. Some of Bill's old groves are still there with housing subdivisions intertwined throughout. Driving around Queen Creek one time, he beamed with pride at the big beautiful homes planted among his citrus trees. He wasn't bragging about the homes; he was proud of the trees, most of which he had personally planted, still thriving after all those years.

Bill used to say, "There is opportunity everywhere; you just have to find it." As he prospered, he was able to play bigger games, moving into real estate investments.

"Buying is easy; it's selling that's the hard part," he would say. "You have to make sure and have a plan for a property when you buy it. Don't just buy something because it's a good deal. What if you have to own it a while? Can it pay for itself?"

Bill liked to buy farms and ranches, because he understood agriculture and could always find something to do with the place until it sold. Later in life he also invested in prime land, building houses.

In the late 1960s, Bill, always an adventurer, sold most of his holdings and bought an entire town in Alaska. Located near Yakutat, the

Bill proudly displays some of his citrus. *Photo by Valerie Juster*

Bill views archeology on his ranch.   *Photo by Valerie Juster*

small town consisted of a fish cannery, store, saloon, boarding house, and a large fishing boat. Other than a few private residences, Bill owned it all. The only way in or out was by air, sea, or sled dogs. It was a rough-and-tumble kind of frontier town straight out of a scene from the century before. Bill even told of once being thrown through the window of his own saloon during a bar fight!

Getting his fill of Alaska after a few years, Bill moved backed to Arizona where he spent the rest of his life cattle ranching, farming, and developing real estate. He owned ranches in New Mexico and Arizona, developed land in pretty much every southwestern state, including the California coast, and even owned a motel in the Arizona resort town of Pinetop for a while.

Bill was constantly helping folks out with financial advice. He also did things like give a buck to the down and out, rides for hitchhikers, and even gave out a free Bible now and then. One time, when he gave financial advice not well received, he was told, "Well that's not the way most people do it." Bill responded in typical Bill fashion, "Let me tell you something: About 10 percent of the people in this country make around 90 percent of the money. So it stands to reason that most of the people are wrong about finances most of the time.

"If you want good advice about money, get it from someone who knows how to make it - I mean *really* knows how to make it. I don't mean someone with a good job, because a job is just a job and with very few exceptions, jobs, even the better paying ones, will never make you rich. If you want sound financial advice, talk to someone who has made themselves a *lot* of money!"

Another thing Bill used to say frequently was, "Anybody in this country has the same opportunity as anyone else. It isn't only the people born into privilege who make it big; actually, it's the opposite most of the time. People who use their background as an excuse will get no sympathy from me. Shoot, I'm living proof; if I can make it, anybody can."

Bill was raised during the Great Depression, rode a horse to school, had parents who struggled financially, and he made every dime he ever had the old-fashioned way: with his own two hands and his ingenuity.

Having several different partners at one time or another on this project or that, Bill always advised against getting too deeply into partnerships, especially with friends or family members. "You still have to have Thanksgiving dinner with them no matter what happens, you know."

But the partner Bill disliked the most was Uncle Sam. "I wouldn't mind the government taking some of my money if they were helping people out with it, but they take more than their fair share, waste most of it, and then give the rest to a bunch of lazy so-and-sos who won't even find a job or help themselves."

"Entitlement" was a cuss word to Bill. Rather, he often used the quote, "The Lord helps those who help themselves."

If he had any regrets, it would be that all those years spent making money and working so hard, he neglected family relations. Bill once said, "Looking back on it now, I can see where I wasn't home nearly enough. My method of being a good husband and father was to make more money and buy them things. I know now that is not the best way. I could have sacrificed a few hours working to spend more time with my family and still made plenty. That's how I would do it, if I had it to do over again."

Bill would often smile when people would say things like, "There just isn't enough time in the day," or "I don't have enough time to get it all done."

He would reply, "Sleep is overrated. You're probably wasting the hours between midnight and 5 a.m." Then he would laugh. There were many years when he was struggling to make it, and he walked that talk. "Sleep a few hours when you get tired, and then get back at it. That's what Edison did."

Bill shook his head in astonishment as he poured over the headlines proclaiming America's consumer debt. "Don't these people know you can never make it if you're drowning in debt?" Then he would explain, "Having and wanting nicer things is the American way. It's what I want too, but you should never buy things that put you into debt. Save the money you have for a down payment and go invest it into something that will make you money instead. Then, later on, you can buy whatever it is you wanted with the profits and still have money to make more money with."

The only acceptable debt to Bill was investment debt - and then you still needed to be careful. "There were times in my life when I didn't know how I was going to get it all covered. Somehow, though, I just kept working at it and believing I could do it, and, sure enough, it always worked out."

Bill Clark (1924–2000) was definitely one of the 10 percent of the population who understood how money is made … really made. He was an American entrepreneur, a great success story, and a great tale of "the American financial dream" realized.

Fry family photo

Richard Fry
Larger Than Life

Richard D. Fry had a zest for life unequalled by most. Many have said, "He was larger than life." Always quick with a smile, a joke, or a story, he was as good-natured as they come. Like all good things, however, they must come to an end ... he passed away on October 5, 2010.

Richard, born in Gatesville, Texas, on January 19, 1949, was a cowboy. Richard's father was a legendary roper and horseman, and the apple didn't fall far from the tree. Richard was raised a-horseback. Growing up, he loved sports (especially football), roping, and good horses; these things held a special place in his life thereafter. He was also what you might call "a people person."

After graduating from college in 1971, with a teaching degree, Richard embarked on a rodeo career in the calf-roping event. Being an avid roper, he always rode good horses (something he was known for his entire life), which added to Richard being a winner. He had a keen way of figuring out how to win, no matter what the game might be. Some folks said he was just naturally lucky, but Richard, like all successful people, knew luck is created.

He roped calves at the professional level from the mid-'70s through the early '80s. One of Richard's favorite stories about calf roping was the year he narrowly missed qualifying for the National Finals Rodeo (NFR). He had faithfully returned home in the fall to work as a math teacher to pay the bills, not realizing until it was too late he had been close enough to being in the top fifteen that a few more rodeos may have been enough to make the finals.

After rodeo, Richard undertook a new journey in life as a racehorse trainer. He did this for over twenty years, during which time he became legendary - not only for his knowledge and ability with horses, but for just plain having a good time as well. As one of the most successful trainers in the Southwest, he was a favorite with celebrities and locals alike in the Jockey Club, where the best parties are thrown. His placing average was almost 40 percent, which is astounding.

Richard was in the "who's who" crowd around racetracks. Then, in 1994, the highlight of his racing career presented itself when he won the All American Futurity at Ruidoso Downs; the world championship of quarter-horse racing. A fast horse named Noblesse Six put Richard in the quarter-horse history books forever. Before retiring as a trainer, Richard became one of the winningest trainers of all time.

In 2004, Richard found real estate sales in his new home state of Arizona. Timing couldn't have been better for the natural-born salesman, as there was a HUGE real estate boom gaining momentum. Just as in other endeavors throughout life, Richard went for the gold with gusto, becoming one of the top real-estate salesmen in his field within a short time, a position he maintained until the end of his days.

Richard was born on a horse. *Photo courtesy of Fry family*

After twenty-six years of retirement from roping, Richard got back into the sport; this time as a jackpot team roper. It didn't take long for him to prove a winner in team roping as well. In the last six years of his life, Richard won dozens of buckles, saddles, and other prizes, not to mention, a boatload of cash. The highlight of his team-roping career came in 2009 when he won the #10 division at the World Series of Team Roping Finale in Las Vegas, Nevada. That win came with a check of over $100,000, but the great thing about that victory was he won it with his lifetime friend, Jim Saunders. (Jim's dad grew up roping with Richard's dad back in Gatesville). After the win, Richard commented that he felt like he'd accomplished just about everything he'd dreamed of at that point, winning the All American and then the World Series: two different equine events and two occasions where he won $100,000 in a day!

Richard spent the last few years of his life traveling around the country to roping events, from Oklahoma City to the California Coast. Along the way he tried to get anyone he came into contact with interested in buying real estate (or anything else he might be selling). Richard had an easygoing way about him, which attracted people. He was also sharp as a tack - smart like a fox.

An avid practical joker, he was constantly giving people a hard time, but normally in subtle ways that made them like it. He was also a heck of a storyteller. Richard had more tall tales than most. Some he would tell just to "See if you'd bite," as he liked to put it. Others were seemingly so bizarre; people would call him on it. Then he'd just say, "Check it out." When they did, they'd find out he wasn't joshing around. Many times when he would tell people about almost making the National Finals in the calf roping event back in the day, people would look at him and say, "Yeah, right."

After all, in his later years, Richard weighed about 300 pounds and looked nothing like an athletic specimen who could rope calves with the best of them. But folks would check it out, and, sure enough, guys like many-time world champion Joe Beaver would verify that Richard was one heck of a roper in his younger days.

Another time, that same Joe Beaver agreed to rope with Richard at the World Series Team Roping Finale in Las Vegas. When Richard would tell people he was roping with Joe at the finale, folks would once again say, "Yeah, right." But sure enough, it was true. People were amazed that a legendary champion would enter a lower level roping with an overweight guy who looked like he couldn't rope a lick. But, as Joe put it, "I'd rope with Richard anywhere. He's a winner." Guess what? They did win a check that year!

Richard loved to have fun and smiled more than anybody. He was definitely "larger than life" in the fun department. With a deep booming voice, which could be heard a mile away, he was the center of attention at gatherings; he thrived on that. After meeting someone for ten minutes, he knew all about them (and vice versa), and they had several friends in common. Nobody could say Richard was bashful.

He went at life full-steam-ahead. A natural risk taker, he won and lost several small fortunes, always bouncing back. One story he liked to tell was about being in Las Vegas during the NFR back when he was still training racehorses. He always played in golf tournaments there, but didn't have much luck at them or at the gambling tables this particular time either. Usually, Richard was the kind of guy who would sit down at the black jack table with a hundred dollars and walk out of there the next morning with $10,000 or more! He'd have a huge crowd gathered around him all night long as he put on a show. This time however, he couldn't get his "mojo" going, and he'd lost every penny - payroll, petty cash, savings; it was all gone.

Richard found an old friend of his and gave him a hot check for $500, telling the friend it wasn't good at the moment, but it would be the first of next week. (He had an uncommon amount of confidence.) Taking the money, he started betting on racehorses - a game he knew more than a little about. After winning a couple thousand on the horses, he returned to the black jack tables, where, by the next morning, he won around $15,000. Come Monday, he was back at the track at Ruidoso Downs, the check written to the friend was good, all business accounts were replenished, and nobody was the wiser. This little story pretty much sums up Richard's go-for-it-all and have fun doing it attitude.

Richard often said, "I don't want to get old." Somehow I think he knew the fast lane, fun-loving lifestyle he lived couldn't accommodate

Richard and Jim win $100,000. Photo by Jennings Photgraphy

old age. I believe he'd rather live sixty-one years as he did rather than eighty or ninety years in a more moderate manner.

Richard was a proud Texan, but also lived a good part of his life in New Mexico and Arizona. He had friends everywhere. In the days following his death, the Fry family was literally inundated with sympathy calls from across the Southwest. He made a big splash in passing just as he did in life.

Richard had an uncommon amount of belief in himself … this belief helped him gain many successes throughout his life. He never thought of himself as inadequate in any way. By the nature of his own thoughts and actions, the stars aligned for him on more than one occasion.

Richard Fry and Ryan Anderson win big! *Photo provided by Fry family.*

Magill family photo

Bill Magill
A *REAL* Cowboy

One of my favorite cowboy heroes and one of Arizona's most colorful cowboys was Bill Magill.

Bill Magill spent most of his life on Arizona cattle ranches, but was actually born near Marathon, Texas, in 1928. He was raised on a ranch there. Bill knew from his earliest memories that the only thing he ever wanted to be was a cowboy. Being raised in south Texas, not far from the Mexican border, Bill learned to speak Spanish at an early age. His mother told him he could speak Spanish before English. All of his playmates at an early age were of Mexican descent. Speaking Spanish proved to be an important and useful tool throughout Bill's life.

Bill grew up, like most ranch kids, with an extensive knowledge of horses and cattle, a love of the outdoors, and anything to do a-horseback. Whether it was a roping competition or "punchin" cows on the open range, he had a great love of adventure.

Coming of age in the late 1940s, one of the best jobs he could dream of was one that combined adventure and livestock. It just so happened about that very time, the United States government was hiring people to go to Mexico and assist the Mexican government with the *Eradicacion de la Fiebre Aftosa* or the Eradication of Hoof and Mouth Disease, as it was known on this side of the border.

Young men from states close to the Mexican border, who could speak Spanish and had a livestock background, were highly sought after for this job. Bill eagerly signed up to become an inspector for the government project. He headed for Mexico with great excitement.

Bill told me he really thought he knew how to speak Spanish while growing up; after all, he could speak with the hands working for his dad with ease. "Well," Bill said, "I just started to learn Spanish the day I touched down in Mexico City." When he got off the airplane, he got a taxi ride to the American headquarters. Along the way he visited with the cab driver and saw right away that he and the driver didn't speak the same lingo.

As it turned out, two years later, when Bill returned to Texas by airplane, that very same cab driver gave him a ride from the American headquarters to the Mexico City airport. Along the way, they visited, and, upon reaching their destination, the driver looked at Bill and told him, "You have really learned to speak good Spanish in the last couple of years." The cab driver had remembered Bill and was now impressed with his knowledge of the language.

Many books have been written about people's experiences while in Mexico on the *Eradicacion de la Fiebre Aftosa*. Bill's experiences could fill one of those books. He and the other inspectors experienced a way of life few Americans ever have, or will. If you get a chance to read a book about that era, I highly recommend it.

When Bill returned to Texas in about 1950, there was a great drought going on. Most people from the Southwest have heard about "the time it never rained" or the drought of the 1950s. Well, times were tough back then and especially tough for people in the livestock business. Because of the drought, there just weren't many cowboying jobs available. Since Bill had fallen in love with Mexico, he decided to return.

He bought a $30 visa, good for thirty days, and returned Mexico. As it turned out, he ended up staying for five years. He used to laugh and say, "I was a 'wetback' on the other side." He said it in a good-natured way, as there was not a prejudicial bone in his body.

While staying in Mexico, Bill worked on several great ranches and lived like a cowboy from the late 1800s or early 1900s might have lived. He rode horseback for almost 100 percent of his transportation and lived in many areas where there were not any roads. He carried a gun for personal protection and slept under the stars a good bit of the time.

He once told of a time when he was foreman for a rancher outside of Chihuahua City. In those days, all the cattlemen in that part of Mexico drove their herds to the city to sell at the railroad depot.

At shipping time this particular year, the ranch hands drove the cattle to Chihuahua according to tradition. After about a one-week cattle drive, the herd and the hands arrived at their destination. The custom of the ranch owner was then to get himself and his foreman (Bill) a room at the big hotel located in the middle of town. It was party central, similar to what Dodge City might have been like in the day of the great trail drives.

When they headed into the hotel, another rancher and his foreman were coming out. As it turned out, there was bad blood between these two ranchers and heated words were exchanged. Bill said he honestly thought he was going to be in an Old West-style gunfight, as all men present were armed with pistols. Nothing wound up happening, but can you imagine being in a real-life situation like that, straight out of an old Western?

Cowboy Bill loved to rope.
Photo by Jim Olson

Bill had the opportunity to experience a way of life that disappeared from the American frontier around the turn of the 1900s. What an amazing thing to be able to do in the 1950s, and live to tell about it in the 1990s! He was like talking to a living witness of the long-ago past.

After Bill came back from Mexico, he drifted around a bit, working here or there, but eventually decided to go further west. You see, that drought of the '50s had been a huge influence on the decision Texas stockmen made to now stock their ranches with sheep and goats. Well, no true cowboy (as Bill Magill was) would stand for much sheep and goat punchin'. He would say, "I had to leave Texas for fear of becoming a sheep and goat herder." Then he would laugh his good-natured laugh and finish with, "That's how I ended up in Arizona."

Moving west turned out to be the right move, and he called Arizona "home" for the rest of his life. Bill loved Arizona and punched cows in most every part of the state. Not long after moving to the state, Bill met the love of his life, Evelyn Savage. They proudly raised four boys and a girl. Those kids grew to become upstanding citizens and all-around genuine people who remain close to their Western roots.

Over the next forty-plus years, while cowboying across the state, Bill made lots and lots of great friends. He was always the kind of guy who had a smile on his face and a kind word for those who deserved it. He was a cowboy from the word "go" and loved everything about the life. He rode rank horses, caught wild cattle in places most people wouldn't dare to hike (much less ride a horse), ran several ranches, worked for several feed yards - just cowboying in general his whole life through. He was one of the last, great, "true" cowboys from an era most of us have only heard or read about.

Bill served as an interpreter on hundreds of occasion in many different situations. He had a unique understanding of the Mexican people that most Americans will never grasp. I remember vividly long visits with Bill at my kitchen table after we had finished riding, roping, or moving cattle. He would tell stories of punching cows, ridin' wild country in far-off places of Mexico, and try to give me an understanding of a different culture.

He could teach Spanish with a knack like no other. He would explain it to you - not just translate words. As a matter of fact, he had a gift for languages, and, after spending time with someone who spoke another language, he would begin to talk back to them in their own native tongue. He also spoke pretty good Apache and Papago (Tohono O'odham) as he spent time cowboying with both.

Just as Bill Magill was born a cowboy, lived his life as a cowboy; he also died a cowboy. Bill passed away on November 22, 2000, from a horse accident at the age of seventy-two. Even though the doctor had told him to give up cowboying years before, you just couldn't keep Bill off a horse. He died the perfect death for a cowboy (if there is such a thing). He was riding a good horse on a crisp beautiful morning while checking pasture cattle to help out a neighbor. The horse slipped and fell in a ditch, and Bill never felt any pain - it happened fast.

Bill's funeral was held in Florence, Arizona. The church was so full, there was standing room only on the inside, and some people had to stand outside, listening on speakers. If all of Bill's friends had been there, they would have needed a good-size rodeo arena to accommodate them all.

Well, that's just exactly what I thought, so on January 21, 2001, I helped organize a memorial team roping and wild cow milking in Bill's honor and to help out the Magill family with expenses. On that Saturday in Casa Grande, Arizona, at the rodeo grounds, people came from all over the state and even the Southwest to join in and remember a great cowboy.

Bill Magill had more friends than anyone I ever saw, and, when Bill's horse was led around the arena with an empty saddle, there wasn't a dry eye in the place. Over 800 teams competed that day in one of the largest ropings ever held in Casa Grande. That should say something about the kind of man Bill Magill was; everyone wanted to be there and pay tribute.

Bill was the kind of fellow who always had a smile on his face and a kind word in his heart. He was also cowboy to the core. Knowing Bill Magill was like knowing a John Wayne character in real life. It was an honor.

Memorial marker where Bill died. Photo by Jim Olson

Jim Olson

Public image, provided by family

Earl Thode

First All-Around Champion

Trevor Brazile has won nine of them (and counting). Ty Murray has won seven. Both Larry Mahan and Tom Ferguson have six. Winning the Professional Rodeo Cowboys Association All-Around Championship proclaims, emphatically, you are the most versatile rodeo cowboy in the world.

Way back in 1929, Earl Thode won the very first World Champion All-Around Cowboy title of professional rodeo. Thode, originally from South Dakota, competed in bull dogging and roping events, but was best known for his classic saddle bronc riding style, an event at which he excelled.

Born on December 7, 1900, he was said to have been riding horses on the family ranch south of Belvedere, South Dakota (not much more than a wide spot in the road), by the age of five. By eleven, he was considered a great rider, riding racehorses at local county fairs. In his teens, he was breaking and training horses for his father and other area ranchers. According to reports, Earl had an uncanny way with horses.

Earl entered his first rodeo, the local White River Stampede, in 1920, where he won the all-around championship—no small deal, as this was a renowned rodeo at the time. For the next seven years he mostly rodeoed around South Dakota and worked as a cowboy. In 1927, he decided to make rodeo his full-time career.

After the Madison Square Garden rodeo finale of '27, Earl and a bunch of other contestants were invited to England to perform for Brit-

Earl on horseback.
Public image, provided by family

ish royalty. In an interview with author Dan Woods, Earl had this to say about riding before the queen, "They made us bronc riders wrap our spurs with rags and wouldn't let us use a quirt. 'Twas quite different from this country, but everyone seemed to enjoy it."

Earl had a unique spurring style (for the times), involving the fore and aft motion from point of shoulder to flank, which all bronc riders are required to use today. He was the first to use this technique, however, and is credited with its invention.

Earl Thode's rodeo resume reads like the "Who's Who" in rodeo: four World Champion Saddle Bronc riding titles (1927, 1928, 1929, and 1931) and one World Champion All-Around Cowboy title (1929). He won all the major rodeos of his day, including Calgary, Madison Square Garden, Fort Worth, Tucson, Phoenix, and Cheyenne, to name a few. He actually won the bronc riding event at Cheyenne four different times, a record held these many years since.

This rodeo legend originally competed in the Rodeo Association of America, which was the predecessor of the Cowboy Turtles Association formed in 1936. In 1945, that organization's name changed to the Rodeo Cowboys Association, and, in 1975, became the Professional Rodeo Cowboys Association, which is what we have today. (He had membership No. 36.) In 1979, Earl Thode was inducted posthumously into the Pro Rodeo Hall of Fame.

It has been written that he probably should have a couple more all-around titles to his credit, but, prior to 1929, records were sketchy. Also prior to '29, the world champion was based upon winning a certain rodeo and not the whole year's accumulation of rodeos. Earl was part of the reason they started keeping track of totals won in two or more events, thereby naming the all-around champion each year.

In 1929, while competing at Calgary, he broke his leg. During his stay in the hospital, he was brought back to health by nurse Edna Blodwen Cole (friends called her "Blodie"). Earl came back to visit Blodie during the Calgary rodeo the following year. The two were married in 1931, when Earl returned once again for the event.

The Calgary Stampede was a special rodeo for Earl: He won several times there; he met his future wife there; and, in 1937, it was where he retired from professional rodeo. After getting banged up by the pickup horse upon dismounting from his bronc, Earl knew bronc riding at age thirty-seven was not in the cards any longer.

Author R. Lewis Bowman, nephew of world champion Everett Bowman, remembers going to rodeos as a kid with his Uncle Everett and meeting the great Earl Thode. The two champions were close friends, but what Lewis remembers most about the champ, was his kindness. "Earl had time for everybody. He would walk up and shake the hand of a kid, smile, and visit a while," says Lewis. "That made him pretty high up in my book as I was about five years old the first time I met him."

Being kind to children was a trademark of the rodeo great. He had two sons of his own, but often took in wayward kids, making his sons feel at times as if they were part of a much larger family. He could have hired cowboys to work on his ranch, but would hire a needy youngster over the more experienced man every time. He was involved in the Elks Lodge and instrumental in the Shriners parades, raising money for children's hospitals. Time and time again, he donated beef to boys' homes anonymously.

It was also reported that Earl was a quiet and humble man, often feeling almost embarrassed at the attention given to him as a world champion and celebrity figure. According to his younger son, former Yuma County Arizona Superior Court Judge Thomas Thode, "There are twelve people named after Pops that I know of and only three of them are blood-related."

In 1934, the Thodes moved to Casa Grande, Arizona where they homesteaded a 320-acre farm and ranch near Eleven Mile Corner. In

Earl rides "Danger Boy"
Public image, provided by family

the late 1930s, Earl and partners leased several parcels of state and private land in the area between Casa Grande and what is now Arizona City, where they ran cattle on the desert during winter months. He eventually bought a ranch west of town on Midway Road in 1941 with proceeds made from the sale of the Eleven Mile Corner place and money made running cattle. The 1,000-plus acres of patented land on Midway became what most old-timers of the area call "the Thode Ranch." He ran cattle and raised cotton there.

Earl was very active in the Fiesta de Los Vaqueros rodeo in Tucson, traveled to New York to direct the Madison Square Garden rodeo several times, and was arena director at the Phoenix rodeo as well. Locally, at the Casa Grande Rodeo Days, he is credited with being the first arena director and committee president, a position he held for many years.

Blodie became active in Arizona politics. She joined the Woman's Club, was elected to the state Legislature an amazing eighteen times, and was instrumental in the formation of the Casa Grande Regional Hospital.

During this time, Earl also bought a ranch at Douglas, where he raised cattle and the family visited in the summer to get out of the desert heat. In the late 1950s, the Douglas ranch was sold, and Thode bought one in the Arizona White Mountains near Vernon, moving most of his ranching operation up there.

On May 18, 1964, Earl was fishing alone in a small boat on a pond at his ranch. He was later found dead. It was determined that the boat capsized, drowning Earl in the chilly water.

To this day, Earl Thode remains a legend in rodeo circles, but, more importantly, his reputation for being a humble, yet generous man, lives on.

John Beckett

Bobbi Jeen Olson

Actress, Model, Cowgirl

One day, an idea came to me! I was flippin' through the channels in search of something worthwhile to watch. (With 250 channels on satellite TV, you'd think it'd be easy, but it's often not.) Then I noticed *The High-Lo Country* was coming on. This is an enjoyable Western movie set in New Mexico in the late 1940s. It stars Woody Harrelson and Sam Elliot among others. I told my young son to watch the beginning with me for a little while. As he watched, Woody Harrelson danced in a barroom scene. My boy looked up at me and said, "Popi [that's what he calls me] that looks like Momma dancing with that man." "Well son," I told him, "that *is* momma dancing with that man."

You see, our son had seen his momma in print ads before, and I guess he had been told that she'd been in movies, but I think actually seeing her on TV like that made it real to him. As he watched with interest, he asked me if Momma had been in other TV movies. "Sure she has," I told him, "she's done a lot of movie and TV work before." I would like to share a little of that history with you all as well.

Bobbi Jeen Olson is very proud of her Western heritage and very enthusiastic about promoting the Western way of life. It all began in her native state of New Mexico. She first became a rodeo queen there in the 1990s; she started at the local level, did well, and progressed to the state level. That experience and the connections made while competing at the New Mexico State Fair led to her "being discovered."

A talent agent found that she was "a natural" in front of a camera and eager to work in movies, TV commercials, and even do stunt work. Soon she was modeling many products, doing modeling/print ads for Western clothing stores, and was even the subject of a popular photo series done by a world-renowned photographer. Today, that photo series is a limited edition (selling for a lot of money). She was on a swimsuit poster, modeled Wrangler Jeans, and was featured in promotional ads.

Besides print modeling, she worked in TV commercials for numerous companies. She also appeared in both country and rock music videos. Her image was filmed, and then used on videos that were then used for CD-ROM games.

She has also done stunt work in Western movies, doubled for and did horseback riding scenes for several famous actresses. She has worked with some of the biggest names in the world of Western stunts. She can drive wagons, shoot from rearing horses, fall from running horses (on purpose of course), and do about any riding scene that your typical Hollywood actress can't or won't do.

Working in movies is a favorite of Bobbi Jeen, and she has appeared in such films as the made-for-TV movie *Stolen Women*, which was filmed entirely on the Kansas plains. Among other things, she did all of the riding scenes in that film for the actress, Jean Louisa Kelly.

She also portrayed Etta Place, who was the real-life girlfriend of Butch Cassidy, in a PBS documentary. That documentary is one of the most popular ones shown when PBS is doing a historical report on Butch and Sundance. Anytime Etta is shown, it is actually Bobbi Jeen.

She has been on *Walker Texas Ranger,* a well-known TV show starring Chuck Norris; the Western TV series *The Lazarus Man*, which starred Robert Urich; a CBS movie-of-the-week called *Scattering Dad*; and, as I mentioned earlier, danced with Woody Harrelson in *The Hi-Lo Country*, which also starred Sam Elliot, Penelope Cruz, and Patricia Arquette. She has rubbed elbows with many of the most famous actors and actresses of our time. In spite of her success and brushes with fame, Bobbi Jeen downplays her roles in the projects she was involved with back then.

Her talents run deeper than looking pretty in ads, doing Western stunts, and acting tough. She is an excellent horsewoman and a highly sought-after team-roping partner at events across the country. Whether

A designer photo shoot with Picsindesign.com

in Amarillo, Texas, or Salinas, California, people take notice of the pretty little redhead who looks like she should be modeling instead of roping.

Bobbi Jeen actually has an extensive background with horses and cattle, and has even trained first-rate cattle dogs. Ranching and the country way of life are deep in her roots. Raised a country girl on a ranch most of her life, she still lives on one today. Even when she is attending a "high dollar" affair where formal is the norm; she is well-known for the "country spin" she brings with her, not only in dress, but in character as well.

She has ridden a tame longhorn steer down the streets of Los Angeles in a Fourth of July Parade (making local headlines). And, as evidence of her generous side, she has helped handicapped children learn how to ride horses in a therapeutic school in New Mexico. She can rope, ride, and brand with the best of them, but can attend a formal "at the Ritz" later that day still looking like a supermodel doing it.

In 1998, Bobbi Jeen moved from New Mexico to Arizona, where she continued to work for some time until she decided to become a mom. In the early 2000s, she took time off to focus her attention on raising her young son. She's extremely proud of her family, and to date, her son has also appeared in several ads himself.

Bobbi Jeen and her husband (yours truly) live on and operate a portion of the old Red River Ranch, which was once owned by "Duke" himself, John Wayne.

After a few years off, she decided to renew her career and began appearing in fashion shows, ads, commercials, TV shows, and feature films once again.

Since going back to work, Bobbi Jeen has appeared in movie/TV projects such as the TV series *MANEATER*; an Animal Planet TV series *I Shouldn't Be Alive*; was featured in a promo for a reality TV series called the *Ultimate Gunfighter*; and also many commercial and print ads; several Internet commercials and infomercials, mostly filmed locally in Arizona and...I think you get the picture.

Bobbi Jeen has also done print/modeling work for many major annual fund-raisers throughout the state, working with well-known local and national photographers. She is the 2012 face of a custom-made Western clothing line and she has graced the covers of several magazines including *Arizona Jackpot* and *Phoenix Magazine*. She has been featured in calendars from 2008 through 2012, always adding her special Western flare. Most photographers with whom she has worked remark that Bobbi Jeen "comes alive" when the lens is pointed her way.

Her resume has made her the subject of several feature stories in magazines and profiles in four different books. One of her most recent projects she is extremely proud of is being the host of *Arizona Country TV*, a positive, family oriented program featuring country music and all things country around Arizona. She will be taking viewers on adventures throughout the state, introducing them to amazing people who make a positive difference, and bringing exciting music and interviews with the Western artists.

Whether with a rope, a branding iron, on a horse, in a movie, commercial, or just looking great in a photograph, she diligently works to keep the Western lifestyle alive. She always puts a positive spin on projects she's involved in and is quick with a smile. Bobbi Jeen has also proven a "small town girl" can follow her dreams and have success without having to compromise character and values. She is first rate at combining ranch with class!

Rearing a horse on set. *Photo by Pat Larkin*

Family photo

Sheri Kennedy

Tomboy or Lady? Both!

I have had the pleasure of knowing Sheri Kennedy since she moved to Arizona's Casa Grande Valley in 2005. Since then, I have gotten to know her well and consider her to be a good friend. In fact, a lot of people around the valley have gotten to know her. Yet, many don't recognize what an accomplished and amazing person she is; she's too humble to brag on herself.

I hear comments from people all the time like: "I saw the results on such and such roping in the paper. By the way, who is this Sheri Kennedy that I keep reading about?" Well, hopefully I can clarify it for those who don't know.

Sheri moved to Casa Grande from California, where she was born and raised, simply because she loves to rope. She had lived within 45 minutes of her hometown of Turlock her entire life until leaving for Arizona's great weather and year-round ropings. Roping wasn't Sheri's first love though. Since she was young, she has always been involved in athletics, enjoying softball, volleyball, golf, and wrestling.

Wrestling? Yes, I said wrestling. Sheri comes from a household where wrestling is king. Her dad was a wrestling coach, and her two brothers are also involved in the sport. They did not encourage Sheri to get into wrestling, however. They thought she should pursue a more "feminine sport." That didn't deter Sheri. In the late '80s and early '90s, women's wrestling was getting recognition; the first world championship for women being held in 1987.

When Sheri discovered there was organized women's wrestling coming to Turlock, she was encouraged to try out by her husband, Burr, who was the high school wrestling coach at the time. (Sheri was the assistant high school wrestling coach.) Well, she tried out, made the team, and, in her first full year of wrestling, she did well enough at the U.S. Nationals to qualify as a member of the U.S. Women's World Olympic Team. Her first world meet (1993), she finished seventh in the world. In 1994, she also made the U.S. Women's World Olympic Team and finished eighth in the world. And when I say "seventh" or "eighth" in the world, I mean the whole wide world, not just in the U.S. She wound up qualifying to be on the Women's Olympic Team four different times.

Sheri says she really enjoyed the competition and the physical fitness that wrestling provided, but she also enjoyed getting to travel the world while on the team. She visited places like France, Norway, Sweden, Denmark, Russia, Bulgaria, Poland, Canada, and Venezuela.

One year, while in Venezuela for the Pan American Games, there was a revolt going on in that country. With more than a bit of an understatement, she said, "It was a little different ... going outside and seeing teenage kids running through the streets with machine guns." The kids with machine guns must have not been too much of a distraction as she finished second at the Pan Am Games that year.

Most of her experiences abroad were quite pleasant though, and she especially liked visiting the castles and old buildings of Europe where there was so much interesting history.

During the late '90s, Sheri made the transition from wrestling to rodeoing. When she did, she brought that same fierce competitiveness with her to the rodeo arena. Starting out, she worked long and hard until she had honed her skills to a level where she felt like she could compete and be a winner. She did not enter a rodeo until she felt like she could win!

During her first year of competing as a breakaway roper, she won the 1998 Rookie of the Year Award and the 1998 year-end championship breakaway roping in the California Cowboys Professional Rodeo Association (CCPRA). Sheri also won the CCPRA's breakaway year-end championship in 1999 and was the reserve champ in 2000.

Sheri Kennedy and Connie Hiatt win average at WPRA finals. *Family photo*

From there, Sheri started to compete at the national level and joined the Women's Professional Rodeo Association (WPRA) in 2000. She qualified for the WPRA finals in breakaway roping, calf roping, and team roping in 2000, 2001, and 2002. She is both a header and heeler, switching ends of a roping bovine quite naturally.

One of her career highlights in the WPRA came in 2002, when she won the team-roping average at the Women's National Finals Rodeo. To put this in perspective, it means she and her partner bested the entire field of the top fifteen teams in the world at that time. This speaks volumes about her talent, especially if you consider she had only been roping for five years at that point.

Since 2002, Sheri has slowed down a bit and predominantly become a "jackpot" roper. If you keep up on the results from the major jackpots around the Southwest, such as those of the United States Team Roping Competition (USTRC), American Cowboys Team Roping Association (ACRTA), and World Series of Team Roping (WSTR), you'll be very familiar with her name, because she is a constant winner.

In her short, but decorated, roping/rodeoing career, she has won a saddle for pretty much each year she has competed. Sheri has won more buckles than she can easily count, and prizes like tack and jackets are plentiful around her home.

Besides being an accomplished roper, Sheri is also very good with animals. She has been successful in training horses and dogs in particular. People from Arizona and all over the Southwest bring horses for her to ride. Not only does she have a knack with young horses, but I do believe she could train a dog to play the guitar if she put her mind to it. Her cow dogs are better trained and can do more tricks than about anybody else's. I guess when Sheri puts her mind to accomplishing something, she has proven she can, and will be, successful at it.

So, if you are one of the lucky people out there who has had the pleasure of getting to know Sheri Kennedy, the next time you hear somebody say, "By the way, who is this Sheri Kennedy gal from Casa Grande that I've been reading about?", you can respond that you just happen to know she's from California and now lives in Arizona, because she loves to rope so much. Tell 'em that she was on the U.S. Women's Olympic Team as a lady wrestler; and that she has done very well at the state and national level as a breakaway and calf roper. By the way, did I mention that she team ropes very, very well!

Sheri is a prime example of a humble champion. Although she works very hard at what she does, you won't hear her bragging about accomplishments. So if you run across a good-looking gal with auburn hair named Sheri, don't let her looks fool ya. She probably can rope better than you, but can also kick your butt if she had to!

Sheri heeling a steer. *Family photo*

Charles Brooks

The Cowgirls Historical Foundation

A Fine Bunch of Ladies

One of the reasons I write is I love to promote the Western way of life and Western heritage. Imagine my delight and admiration upon hearing about a group of cowgirls from the desert southwest who belong to an organization, whose mission statement includes the phrase "serving as ambassadors, through education and advocacy, of western heritage and the equestrian way of life."

I am referring to a group of ladies known as the Cowgirls Historical Foundation.

It is an understatement to say, "These ladies *stand out* in a crowd." If you see these smiling, friendly, young ladies in their '40s-era period clothing, you will notice they are all stellar examples of proper, young Western women, much the same as, say, Dale Evans was. They are a sight to see and besides "lookin' sharp," they are promoting the Western way of life for the benefit of us all.

The Cowgirls Historical Foundation is a non-profit organization made up of volunteers with a western/equestrian background. They fulfill their organization's mission by being involved in events such as parades, rodeos, educational programs, civic events, and other volunteer activities.

These cowgirls annually attend (and are a part of) the Tournament of Roses Parade held New Year's Day in Pasadena, California. The Cowgirls Historical Foundation is one of about eighteen equestrian entries allowed into the parade. Now, being one of eighteen may not sound like such a big deal, but consider that literally thousands of horse-related groups across the country apply to be one of those, and you gain some respect and appreciation for what being chosen actually means.

Beside the Rose Parade, these women are also involved in other such notable parades as the Fiesta Bowl Parade, Gilbert Days Parade, Prescott Frontier Days, Payson Parade, and many others. The ladies lend their horsemanship skills to rodeos as flag bearers, drill teams, and to introduce events.

Education is important for everyone. More importantly, to us in the West, it's important that the youth of today learn cowboys and cowgirls are real living people caring for the land and animals—a tradition, which needs to continue. The Cowgirls Historical Foundation sends its members out regularly to educate predominately "city" kids on the advantages of equine involvement and the Western way of life.

These fine ladies are involved in civic events as well. If you attend functions such as the National Day of the Cowboy, The High Noon Western Collectible Show, The Festival of the West, certain charity auctions, and numerous other civic and fund-raising events, you will see the representatives of the Cowgirls Historical Foundation there in period clothing promoting our heritage.

These young ladies have spent, and spend, thousands of hours volunteering their services as Western ambassadors each year at events to help raise funds for cancer victims and underprivileged women, among other noteworthy causes. They take that responsibility just as seriously as being in the spotlight of the cameras at the big parades.

One thing aiding these ladies to stand out at events is the period Western clothing and tack they use. A closer look will tell you most of their outfits are similar to those worn by Western performers from the 1940s and '50s. Their authentic outfits are collector's items from famous designers such as Nudie Cohen, Nathan Turk, and Manuel. While these names may be unfamiliar to some, just know that these are the people who designed Western outfits for Roy Rogers and Dale Evans, Gene Autry, Porter Wagner, Ronald Regan, Glen Campbell, and many more. Do the words "Rhinestone Cowboy" come to mind?

The clothing has to be handled with extreme care. After all, when the ladies are wearing them, they are wearing "history." As a matter of fact, a 1950 Rose Parade Marshal (known only at this time as Miss Minton) rode next to Dale Evans in the parade and wore one of the very outfits a Cowgirls Historical Foundation member had the honor of wearing over fifty years later!

The tack these cowgirls put on their horses is no less impressive than their outfits. Saddles from the 1920s through the 1950s are commonplace with the ladies. Bits by Fleming and Garcia, and saddles from Bohlin, Flowers, and Nudie Cohen (including a rare Nudie saddle that is one of only two—the other being on display in the Cowboy Hall of Fame) are what you may see on their horses.

To be a member of the Cowgirls Historical Foundation is an honor to each of its members. But without the truly authentic and unique background of each and every individual person, the Cowgirls Historical Foundation would not be nearly what it is has become. Each member brings her own special contribution to the group.

There are rodeo queens, western models, rodeo champions, horse trainers, a trick roper, rodeo entertainers, horse judges, a Miss Rodeo USA, AQHA show champions, academic honorees, trail riders, ranch hands, and on and on and on among the group of talented horse-

Photo by Charles Brooks

women. Yet, you won't see any of them "showing off" or trying to be the center of attention, as they are all trying to draw attention to their cause as one large group.

There are over twenty members at this time, each from a very diverse background. But when they put on those vintage outfits and saddle up their horses with Western collectables, they become one strong voice for the Western way of life.

This is a very talented, beautiful, friendly, and charming bunch of young ladies. They and their board of directors are great spokespeople for all of us who own a horse or have a Western heritage.

Courtesy of Heidi Durant

Heidi Durant-Payne

Actress, Roper, Teacher

Go to about any major team-roping event across the Southwest, and one of the people you are liable to take note of is a pretty blonde lady riding amongst the run-of-the-mill, scruffy, team ropers. Chances are this lady is Heidi Durant-Payne. She has competed at one time or another in most every major team-roping event from New Mexico to California … even beyond.

What catches your eye first, of course, is the obvious: You don't see pretty blondes roping and riding like that most any ol' day. What gets your attention next, however, is something you may not expect. More often than not, you will see her going to the pay window, collecting a winning check. Yes, Heidi wins more than your average roper. She is a highly sought-after partner at many a major team-roping event.

She always has a positive attitude, a smile, and is friendly to those around her. You have to be impressed with this down-to-earth lady who ropes so well, but, until you get to know her, you don't even realize what a truly amazing (and accomplished) woman you've just met or with whom you've roped.

Heidi was raised in sunny Southern California, near the Los Angeles area. Her parents, Don and Trudy Durant, are pretty amazing people themselves. Many may remember the old Western series *Johnny Ringo*. This was Aaron Spelling's first directing job, and the *Johnny Ringo* series got an honorable mention at Mr. Spelling's memorial when he passed on ... it was that big of a deal!

Well, Johnny Ringo was played by none other than Don Durant. The series ran for several years during the late '50s and early '60s, being quite successful. Don was a talented performer who played the guitar, sang, and acted. He was in several TV shows besides *Johnny Ringo*, such as *The Twilight Zone*. He also did quite a bit of modeling. It was during a commercial shoot that Don met Trudy Roe who wound up being the love of his life. The two lived long and happily together from then on. Trudy also had quite a resume, being a top model herself.

Don Durant had been raised, and lived through, many hard times. So as money came in from acting and modeling, he played it smart, and saved the money made from performing, investing in Southern California real estate. What a right move that turned out to be. Don and Trudy have since passed on, but Heidi remains very fond and proud of her successful parents.

Even though Heidi's parents were successful, she wasn't spoiled or pampered. She attended a public school. She also never gave it a second thought when some directors from a teen magazine came to her high school searching for a model. They held auditions all day, and most every girl in school tried out, hoping to "be discovered" - most every girl that is except Heidi.

She had been around performers and the famous her whole life and thought nothing of it. At the end of the day, as Heidi was walking to the parking lot, one of the directors spotted her and chased her down to ask her to audition for the job. Ironically, the next month, Heidi appeared on the cover of nationally known *Teen Magazine*. I guess you might just say it was "in her genes" to be an actress and model. She was 16 years old at the time and the rest, as you might say, "is history."

Shortly thereafter, she got an agent and for several years she enjoyed a successful acting and modeling career. She is perhaps best known for her part in the television show *Reasonable Doubts*, which also starred Mark Harmon. *Reasonable Doubts* ran for a few years during the mid-'90s, and Heidi was a featured cast member on the show right along with Harmon. She has also appeared on other well-known shows, such as *Baywatch*, *The Adams Family*, *Murphy's Law*, *Clean Slate*, and *General Hospital* to name a few.

Besides being an actress appearing in film and television, Heidi also appeared in commercials and modeled in print ads. She's done a Coca Cola commercial with Joe Namath; commercials for Chevrolet and Slim Fast; and appeared on the covers of *Teen*, *Seventeen*, *Mademoiselle*, and *Surfer* magazines. She has a long list of successful achievements in both film and print, but she is much too modest to brag about it at a team roping. If you were to visit with her and ask, "What do you do?" she would probably reply, "I'm a teacher."

Teaching has always been a passion of Heidi's. She studied it in college, and it's something in which she takes a lot of pride. When the hustle and bustle of acting life began to wear on her, she turned to her first true career choice - teaching. Heidi became a fourth-grade teacher at Agua Dulce Elementary School near where she lived in Southern California.

When asked about her successes as an actress, Heidi downplays them, quick to change the subject. She would rather tell you about the time she had this particularly "tough student" in her class. This kid

Heidi heading a steer during competition.   Photo by Brenda Allen

was, shall we say, "challenging" to put it mildly. When this student went through elementary school, however, he had the good fortune of having Heidi as his teacher. She spent extra time with him and made him believe in himself. As it turned out, he graduated the valedictorian of his class some years later.

During his valedictorian speech, this former "tough student" credited his elementary school teacher (Mrs. Durant) as being the most influential person in his life up to that point. He said without her believing in him, there's no telling where he'd be today. Heidi says teaching was always her "true calling."

Fortunately, for those ropers lucky enough to get to rope with her, she has the same successful drive built into her when competing at her favorite hobby of team roping. As mentioned earlier, Heidi is a highly sought-after partner at major ropings across the Southwest—and with good reason. She's a winner.

When asked about her successes as a roper, she's proud to mention several wins - wins that don't come easily. She has won big at ropings such as The City of Industry (three times) and The Madonna Inn (California); Laughlin, Scottsdale (Lasso Del Sol), Desert Hills, Flagstaff, and Apache Gold (San Carlos) in Arizona; and the Southwest finals at Albuquerque, New Mexico; just to name a few. She has also done well in the Women's Team Roping Association (an all-women's association in California and Nevada); an accomplishment she says was not easy.

Although Heidi has had an interest in horses her whole life, she has only been roping since the late '90s. Before that, she rode English-style, competing in jumping and dressage events.

Back when she had only been roping for a short time, she had an accident with her hand in the rope, losing a portion of one finger in the process. Lots of people would have given up after such a setback, especially Hollywood model types, but not Heidi. She's not like that. She turned the tragedy into fuel to light her fire for even greater success.

She works hard at roping and has taken lessons from some of the best in the business, including Bobby Hurley, Ricky Green, and Shawn Howell. She credits Shawn with a lot of her success. They were neighbors for many years, and he helps keep her and her horses "tuned up" on a regular basis.

When you ask ropers around the Southwest about Heidi, you'll hear comments like "She has such a positive attitude," or "She is so nice to visit with." But remember, when she shows up at a roping, she means business, is known as a winner, and has no problems finding partners.

The next time you are at a major team-roping event around the Southwest, odds are you may run into Heidi. Go over and introduce yourself; she's easy to visit with. And if you are lucky enough to get to rope with her, we'll probably see ya at the pay window.

Fun, outgoing, smart, kind, down-to-earth, ropes well, has great respect for God—all descriptions thrown around when asked to describe Heidi. She is a humble person who knows how to keep success and brushes with fame from going to her head.

Courtesy of Kim Williamson

Kim Williamson

World Champion Cowgirl

Kim Williamson is an eight-time world champion in the Women's Professional Rodeo Association (WPRA). Her successes in the rodeo arena have received coverage in places like *The Western Horseman*, *Super Looper Magazine*, *Loops Magazine*, and *Spin to Win* to name a few. She is a fierce competitor who works hard and has been successful because of it.

However, things have not been easy for her along the way. As a matter of fact, she has faced situations where a weaker-minded person would have just given up, coasting through life as an "average Jane." Not Kim Williamson. She has a positive, persevering go-hard-all-the-way type of attitude in her approach to life and roping.

Kim was born and raised in Farmington, New Mexico, in the beautiful Four Corners area. She enjoyed a well-balanced, happy upbringing there. Kim's dad, Doyle, worked in the booming oil industry and provided well for his family.

Kim says she's always been a "daddy's girl." Doyle bought Kim her first horse when she was eight years old. From that moment, she developed a love for horses. She started going to junior rodeos, enjoying a very successful junior and high school rodeo career.

During her formative years, she traveled the state of New Mexico, winning her first saddles and buckles. Kim qualified for the National High School Finals in barrel racing and breakaway roping events on several occasions.

Then, in 1987, just after Kim's return from the National High School Finals, it happened: Kim's dad informed her he was going to have to sell her horse. You see, in the late '80s, the oil business in the United States went bust. Things like rodeo horses, fancy trucks and trailers, travel expenses, and entry fees were luxuries that could no longer be afforded. Doyle held on long enough to allow Kim to enjoy her high school rodeo career without worry, delaying the bad news as long as he could, but afterward, Kim was just going to have to go out and get a job. He recommended she put herself through college.

After this happened, she just hung around Farmington, wondering what the heck had happened. One minute she had the world by the tail, and the next it seemed like she had nothing. That was quite a setback for a teenager, but Doyle hadn't raised Kim to be a quitter.

It was then she decided to make a move to the Phoenix, Arizona, area. She enrolled in the Devry Institute. Graduating with a bachelor's degree in business operations in 1993, she then set out to make a life of her own. While going to school, Kim and a partner had started Global Services of Arizona, a courier service. She put that same drive and work ethic she had learned from her dad and on the high school rodeo trail into her new business venture.

Global Services of Arizona became very successful, allowing Kim to eventually get back into the rodeo scene. As her business became more successful, she started once again to buy horses, then a truck and trailer, and eventually practice cattle. She fully expected to meet or exceed the level of success enjoyed during her junior rodeo days. And she did.

Kim first went back to rodeoing in Arizona and after a while expanded to New Mexico. During the mid-'90s, she was a competitor at both the Southwest Professional Rodeo Association (SPRA, which later became the GCPRA) and the New Mexico Rodeo Association (NMRA) finals. Life was good once again. She had a successful business and was a successful "weekend warrior" on the amateur rodeo circuit.

It was around this time Kim decided that being a "weekend warrior" was not satisfying her competitive needs on the rodeo trail. She sold her share of the courier business, deciding she would rather ride horses and rope for a living.

By then, Kim was successful enough with rodeo accomplishments that people wanted her to ride horses for them. They knew what kind of "hand" she had become. Just as with the courier business, Kim took her horse riding business to a highly successful level. She started out riding horses for a few dollars per month. Within a short time, she was able to raise her fee considerably and had to hire helpers to keep up with demand. She was just as busy as she wanted to be; everyone wanted her to "tune" their horses up for them.

This took Kim's roping to a whole new level. When you ride horses all day for a living, it's just natural you will also spend a big part of that day roping. Kim was roping 75 to 100 head of practice cattle per day during the week and then going to rodeos on weekends. Well, all that practice sure did pay off, because Kim was a regular at the year-end finals. Then, in 2000, Kim won her first world championship in Women's Professional Rodeo in the team-roping "heeling" event.

Once again, it came to a point where Kim's desire to compete and rope for a living weighed heavily on her decision to get rid of a successful "job." She basically quit riding horses for other people and concentrated full time on roping. Her list of accomplishments is quite lengthy, but all of that roping eventually started taking a toll on her body.

First she started having shoulder and knee problems. This set her back in 2001 and 2002. She wasn't able to compete at a world champion's level and that bothered her. A lot of people may have just hung it up at this point and gone home, satisfied with a successful rodeo career to date, but not this cowgirl. She rehabbed and battled back and, in 2003, was the Reserve World Champion in Team Roping "heading" in the WPRA.

This fired Kim's competitive desire to a new level. Once again starting to practice - roping 75 to 100 head per day. The practice paid off big-time because in 2004, she won three world championships in the WPRA: the all-around, heading and breakaway roping. In 2005, she won four world championships in the WPRA: the all-around, tie down calf roping, breakaway roping, and heeling. That feat put her in the record books as the only woman ever to win back-to-back world championships as both a header and as a heeler! Now Kim had a total of eight world championships (along with three reserve world championships), and it seemed like she had the world by the tail once again.

It's impressive that she competes in four different events. That speaks volumes of Kim's work ethic to have been able to stay competitive against competitors who most often specialize in a single event. Being competitive in four events is what led to her becoming the All-Around World Champion on two different occasions. Staying competitive in those different events has also placed her among the elite ropers of our time. In Men's Professional Rodeo, you think of Ty Murray when contemplating the best all-around rough-stock cowboy, and you have to say Trevor Brazile when commenting on the best men's all-around roper. Of course, you have to think of Kim Williamson when talking about one of the best all-around women ropers.

Just as before, however, the long hours of practice had taken its toll. She was stricken with severe back pain. Add that to the previous knee and shoulder problems and you might just assume that, this time, she would give up on rodeo and go home.

Well, that's just not in her character ... ever. During the latter '00s, she worked hard on taking care of her body and even harder on the mental aspect of her roping.

Kim competes in tie down roping.   Photo by fotoman

Over the years, she also picked up a new occupation—that of a roping instructor—and she puts on several clinics each year. She feels like helping others also helps keep her sharp. As she goes through the basics with her students, it reminds her that roping isn't rocket science. She really enjoys the clinics and has traveled America (even to Australia) while teaching people how to rope ... and be winners.

She feels if her students get just one thing out of her clinics they can take home and put to use in their own roping or their everyday lives, she has achieved success. Some of the things she stresses at her clinics are: the basics of roping (do the little things well and everything else falls into place); a positive attitude; try and try again (and when you think you're done, try some more); have fun; and be thankful each and every day that you're blessed in life. Kim says that life is too short to worry about bad stuff.

One thing she is very proud of is the different horses she rides. She got to be pretty handy with horses during those years she trained them for other people. Kim has had some of the greatest horses in rodeo. On top of that, she either trained them by herself or, at least, keeps them tuned up on her own. Her bay calf-roping horse, Cutter, is perhaps her most famous. He has carried Kim to most of her world championships and was the 2002 "tie down" horse of the year in the WPRA. Besides Cutter; Blue, Roany, and Gray Mare have also helped her achieve world championships.

Kim suffered another major setback in early 2007, when she lost her best friend and mentor, her dad Doyle. Losing Doyle left a big hole in her heart. He had always been there for her, pushing her to be the best at whatever she was doing. This setback, just like others before, didn't keep Kim down for long. She has a positive, winning, aggressive attitude about her roping and life in general, and that's been a major factor in her success to date.

We can all learn a lesson from this eight-time world champion. Her positive, aggressive, "go git em" attitude is an inspiration and prime example of how to become a winner no matter the odds.

Jim Olson

Sharlot Hall Museum (public image)

Sharlot Hall

A Woman Ahead of Her Time

She was the first woman to hold public office in the Arizona Territory and way ahead of her time with regard to being an independent woman. She was Arizona's first real historian preserving the history of early frontier days from the territory. Poet, writer, rancher, friend of many of the day's leading citizens, and humanitarian as well. Her name was Sharlot Hall.

Sharlot came to the Arizona Territory as a young girl in a covered wagon during 1882; she was eleven. Arizona remained her home until her death in 1943. In between those years is the storied life of an amazing lady.

By default, she was a rancher. Her family raised horses and other livestock, grew vegetables, apples, and pears, and her father even tried his hand at gold mining in nearby creeks. Eventually the family settled near what is now Dewey, Arizona, on a place they named Orchard Ranch. Sharlot spent close to 40 years at Orchard Ranch, burying both parents there in the process. The hardships of pioneer ranch life were a common theme in her later writings.

In 1906, there was a measure before Congress to bring both the Arizona and New Mexico territories into the union as one state—the state of New Mexico. Sharlot was one of many activists who opposed the measure. She toured the territory, gathering signatures for a petition against it. During this time, Sharlot was inspired to write her epic poem, "Arizona." The poem was widely accepted as a fine work of art, and a copy of it was distributed to every member of Congress back in Washington, D.C. It has been speculated that the bill was defeated, in part, because of Sharlot's activities and poem. Arizona became its own state in 1912.

In 1909, Sharlot became the first woman to hold a paid public office in Arizona - that of official territorial historian. It ruffled the feathers of many of the day's politicians, as it was unheard of for a lady to hold such a post. Women didn't even have the right to vote in Arizona at that time. Many of her male counterparts searched in vain for a loophole that would legally remove her from her office.

Luckily, the governor of the territory, Richard Sloan, was an ally of Sharlot's and didn't give in to the political pressure from his constituents. It wasn't until George Hunt became the first governor of the newly formed state of Arizona in February 1912, that Sharlot was removed from her post. Hunt may not have been a fan of women in office ... or perhaps he gave into the political pressures his predecessor avoided.

Sharlot remained active in Arizona politics however, and, in 1925, when Calvin Coolidge was elected president of the United States, Sharlot was commissioned to deliver Arizona's three electoral votes to Washington on behalf of the state.

Being an independent woman was a trademark of Sharlot's. She didn't receive a lot of schooling as a young lady (only about four years of formal education), but she quickly learned that young ladies of the day were mostly groomed on how to be a good wife. Sharlot dreamed of being a writer instead.

According to Margaret Maxwell, Sharlot's biographer, she sold her first article for two dollars as a sixteen-year-old while attending Prescott High School. Throughout her life, she had over 500 published works including ten books. Two of her most famous books are *Cactus and Pine* and *Poems of a Ranch Woman*. She was a prolific writer.

As a teenaged girl, while strolling the streets of Prescott with her mother, Sharlot told her mother, "One day I shall live in that fine mansion." She was referring to the old governor's mansion on Gurley Street, home of the first territorial governor, built in 1864.

Sharlot either had extrasensory perception or one heck of a positive, goal-orientated attitude, because, in 1927, she did move into that very mansion. She lived there the rest of her life. From that day on, she dedicated herself to preserving the history of the territory through the formation of a museum - a museum, which to this day bears her name. She was completely enthralled with history.

She had spent most of her life collecting artifacts, studying, and preserving history. Even during her younger life, she knew there was a need for such endeavors, as the old pioneers and their ways were giving way to modern society. President Abraham Lincoln signed legislation to form the territory in 1863, but by as early as 1900, the first pioneers were dying off. Their possessions were being lost along with their stories. To save what she could, Sharlot began collecting Native American and pioneer material. Today, the Sharlot Hall Museum covers 3.5 acres in downtown Prescott and is one of the West's most complete collections of Old West history.

One thing that impresses me most about Sharlot was her independence. Being raised in a time when women were largely thought of as incomplete without a husband; an era when basically the only "career women" were cooks, laundresses, and schoolteachers, and then only if they were single; she was a renegade.

Sharlot at the Governor's mansion.
Public image courtesy of Sharlot Hall Museum

She never married, and once wrote this about the subject: "I am a woman a full ten years beyond thirty. I am not married. I don't expect to be married. I don't want to be married. I am happier than any married woman I have ever known. My 'Emotional Life' is fuller in every direction than that of any wife of my acquaintance. Unless an unmarried woman is a hopeless lump of stupidity, she has a hundred times wider opportunity for an emotional life, full to overflowing, than it is possible for an ordinary married woman to have."

Needless to say, many of her acquaintances were men. She lived in, thrived in and conducted business in a man's world. She was acquainted with most of the leading citizens of her day, including many historical figures whose names sprinkle history books. In response to a male friend's telegraph, inquiring about her welfare, as she was without a husband, Sharlot sent the following reply telegram:

"But I do enjoy everything - just the sunshine on the sand is beautiful enough to keep one giving thanks for eyes to see with. And all

Governor's mansion as it is today at Sharlot Hall Museum. Photo by Jim Olson

day long I'm glad, so glad, so glad that God let me be an out-door woman and love the big things. I couldn't be a tame house cat woman and spend big sunny, glorious days giving card parties and planning dresses - though I love pretty clothes and good dinners and friends - and would love a home where only the true, kind, worth-while things had place. I'm not unwomanly - don't you dare to think so - but God meant woman to joy in his great, clean, beautiful world - and I thank Him that He lets me see some of it not through a windowpane. Your telegram came yesterday - on from Phoenix. Every one of my happiest thoughts, all the days through, ends in a prayer for you - and gratitude beyond words that I have you to call friend - dear, dear, dear Great Comrade. Goodnight, Amigo, God keep you everywhere. S. M. H."

That does not mean, however, that she didn't have female friends. It has been reported that her best friend and closest confidant was Alice Hewins, who wrote a brief biography on Sharlot. "Sharlot was particularly gifted to tell the woman's side of pioneer life. Her warm sympathies, her gift of expression and having lived most of her life under pioneer conditions particularly qualified her." Alice's description seems to fit nicely.

I believe that, in a way, Sharlot Hall paved the way for every woman who has come along since and been successful in a so-called "man's world." She was certainly one of the first to prove it could be done.

Jim Olson

David Sutton (with permission)

Duke and Louie

A Partnership for the Ages

In the late 1950s, American icon John Wayne bought into a 4,000-acre cotton farming operation near Stanfield, Arizona, on the advice of his financial advisor. In a short time, the famous actor knew he was in trouble; he was losing his shirt in the cotton farming business. His financial advisor, who was running the farm, didn't know any more about farming cotton than John Wayne did - maybe even less. Wayne needed to do something about his farm, and he needed to do it soon.

Throughout John Wayne's life, it has been said he strived to surround himself with the best in the business. As he gained prestige and could command more control in movies which he acted in, he demanded more and more that certain people be involved. John Wayne is well-known for having a certain group of confidants he worked with over and over in the movie industry. These were people who Wayne had worked with in the past. He trusted them. He got along with them.

Louis Johnson started farming cotton in 1939, before he turned 20 years old. Louis had grown up around cotton; his family was involved in the business. When he started growing cotton on his own, however, he wasn't happy with his production results.

Louis then asked around about who the best cotton farmer in the area was. Once he found out, he went and hired that man as a manager. Soon he had the yields he wanted, not to mention the knowledge as well. Louis Johnson was another successful man who always sought

Duke looks over the Hereford Bulls. Photo by David Sutton (with permission)

to surround himself with the best in the business. By the late 1950s, Louis Johnson had been unofficially dubbed by many as "the world's champion cotton grower."

On one hand, you have John Wayne, who always surrounded himself with the best people he could, helping to make him successful on the big screen. On the other, you have Louis Johnson, who always hired the best help available in the farming business and became a highly successful cotton farmer. Both men were also very hard workers; that's another important ingredient to success. The two had similar ways of thinking, and their levels of success were second to none (even though John Wayne's success was obviously more visible).

When Wayne noticed he was losing a lot of money farming, he wanted to replace his farm management. As fate would have it, when he asked around about who the best in the business might be, he was told to contact Louis Johnson, who happened to own the farm next door.

At first Johnson turned down the offer to manage Wayne's farm, simply because he was already busy enough. Later, however, the two men had a long visit and got along wonderfully. It was then "Louie," as "Duke" always called him, finally agreed to manage the actor's cotton farm for one year. The two agreed upon a pay scale that had bonuses for certain performance levels that might be reached at harvest time. Louie got the highest possible bonus at the end of that first year, and Duke made a lot of money farming for the first time. It was a match made in heaven, and soon thereafter, Duke proposed a partnership.

At the time, Louie was farming 6,000 acres of primarily cotton ground near Stanfield with Duke's 4,000 acres right next door. The two agreed on a partnership, and before it was said and done, the Red River Land Company as it became known was increased to a 14,000-acre operation.

That's not where the story ends; before it was all over, the partnership owned an 85,000-head cattle-feeding operation known as Red River Feedlot and an 800-head purebred Hereford cattle ranch known as 26 Bar. Both men had a flair for doing things in a big way, and both had a code which said, "If it's worth doin', then do it right."

On the farming side, Louie ran the operation like a well-oiled machine. With an operation that large, he broke it down, managing it as several smaller units, each with its own foreman and set of workers. As per his character, he hired the best help he could find. Louie himself made the rounds every day during the working season and saw to it that he visited each and every field at least once a day; sometimes two or three rounds were necessary. He rose well before daybreak. The industrious Louie wore out a pickup about every six months. He was definitely a hands-on type of farmer; he didn't run the operation from a distance. Duke visited when he could.

In the beginning, Red River Land Co. was primarily a cotton farm. With Louie at the helm, good managers in place, irrigators, tractor drivers, mechanics, and so on, Red River was a moneymaking operation. It was a good arrangement that suited both Duke and Louie. Then, in the early 1960s, an event happened that led the partnership into new directions.

It was then the government put limitations on the amount of acreage that could be planted in cotton. Large irrigated farms like Red River were producing way too much cotton, so the government placed limitations upon them in an attempt to control price and production. Not to be deterred, the partners agreed on another plan for their operation. Enter Red River Feedlot.

On acreage that could not be planted in cotton, Red River Land Co. started to grow alfalfa and small grains for cattle feed. At first an 18,000-head grower yard was built where cattle were backgrounded before being sent to finishing feedlots where they then went for butcher. After about three years of that, however, the feedlot was expanded once again.

In preparation, Louie toured all major feedlots he could get to for ideas. Then Red River was expanded to an 85,000-head capacity with a state-of-the-art feed mill. Cattle could now be finished out right there without having to leave. Red River feedlot was credited as being the largest and most modern privately owned feedlot in the country at the time. Keeping true to form, the best management, cowboys, feed workers, and office help were hired to work at Red River Feedlot. It became another successful venture for Duke and Louie.

During the feedlot building years, the two men talked about it and agreed they wanted to get into the purebred cattle business as well. Just as with everything else they did, they studied on it and decided to do it the best way they felt possible. They wanted to raise the best cattle available at the time and also to own the best ranch in the country. That is what led them to decide on the Purebred Hereford business and eventually to the 26 Bar ranch.

It took some doing, but eventually Duke and Louie were able to put together 14 different properties near Springerville, Arizona, which became the 26 Bar ranch. It consisted of 20,000 deeded acres and another 30,000 acres of forest grazing lease. It ran 800 head of cows and the famous 26 Bar brand came as part of the deal. (The brand was the 99th brand registered in the state of Arizona!) As I said, those two guys believed in doing things in a big way once they committed to a project. The 26 Bar ranch is one of the most beautiful spots in the entire West and, according to those who worked on the ranch, was one of the most productive as well.

The registered Hereford cattle were bought from all of the top breeders at that time. Duke and Louie went to ranches and sales all across the country looking for the best cattle. While they were at it, they also hired a manager and other herdsmen from those same reputable Hereford breeders. Keeping with their theme, they bought the best from the

Duke, Louie and herdsman at 26 Bar Ranch. *Photo by David Sutton (with permission)*

best and hired the best help possible. Soon, another successful venture had been added to their ever-growing estates.

Naturally, when you are in the purebred business, you need a method for marketing your cattle. That's how the 26 Bar's sales got started. Each year in November on the weekend after Thanksgiving, there was a 26 Bar purebred Hereford bull sale held at the partnership's headquarters near Stanfield. The bull sales started in the late 1960s and went on for 18 consecutive years thereafter. These sales were quite festive events, and no corners were cut in the planning of them. They were as much a social event as they were a method to market fine Hereford cattle. People came from far and wide to buy Hereford cattle from one of the best herds in the country. According to records and statements from the Hereford association, the 26 Bar sales were among the highest grossing sales in the country.

Over the years, the partnership of John Wayne and Louis Johnson literally made millions of dollars. Both men have been quoted as saying they never had a disagreement; not only were they great business partners, but they were the best of friends. The two men were equal partners, and Louie worked as the general manager. He worked his tail off at Red River and 26 Bar, while Duke worked like a driven man making movies. The arrangement suited them fine.

Louie and Duke at 26 Bar Bull Sale, Stanfield, AZ. Photo by David Sutton (with permission)

While Louie is credited with managing the day-to-day operations, Duke was also involved, mostly from a public relations and marketing standpoint. He was briefed on the goings on periodically. He knew the breeding of the purebred cattle, the number of cattle owned in the feedlot, and the yields of cotton produced. Duke has been quoted as saying that he trusted Louie completely, and, until his death, he never missed attending one of the sales.

This well-known partnership only came to an end when John Wayne died on June 11, 1979. It probably would be going on today if the two were still alive. In about 20 years of being partners and friends, they had amassed around 34,000 acres of deeded land, another 30,000 acres of leased land, one of the finest cattle herds in the country, and a large feedlot operation.

Duke and Louie came into this world without any money, being brought up by humble, middle class families. Both of them left this world as very wealthy men. As a testament to their success, when the operations were sold in 1980 to settle the estate of John Wayne, it was reported to be the highest grossing farm and ranch sale in the state of Arizona to that date. Hard work and perseverance definitely paid off for these two.

Jim Olson

Dale Smith

World Champion … Everything

Dale Smith moved to Stanfield, Arizona, from the Chandler, Arizona area in December of 1988, because of its great central location. Being in the horse and rodeo business, he could easily move about the state and country from his new home. Not only did Stanfield have a great location, but it was "pleasing to me," as Dale put it. He had purchased 100 acres and the ranch house from Dennis and Linda Nowlin, which was part of the old Red River Ranch. (Linda is the daughter of John Wayne's partner, Louis Johnson, see previous chapter.)

Dale was born in Safford, Arizona, in 1928. He first became famous through rodeo, rising to stardom in the 1950s on the professional rodeo circuit. He was the first man to qualify for the "Super Bowl of Rodeo," the National Finals Rodeo (NFR), in three different events (team roping, calf roping, and single steer roping). Dale was a two-time World Champion, (1956 and 1957) in the team-roping event and runner-up in 1954 and 1958. He was also runner-up in the World Championship in calf roping in 1959 - by less than fourteen dollars. In all, Dale wound up with twenty NFR qualifications. His storied rodeo career continued right on up through the 1990s. Dale even tied a calf in 10.5 seconds on his sixty-fifth birthday to win a Senior Pro Rodeo at Quartzite, Arizona!

Perhaps Dale became most famous in those early years for yet an-

Dale and Poker Chip, a winning combination. Photo courtesy of Smith family

other reason. Arguably, he owned one of the best roping horses ever - the famous Poker Chip. He first acquired Poker Chip in 1955, when he was a five-year-old. In a period between 1955 and 1963, Dale won over $125,000 in prize money on Poker. (That does not count jackpots or open shows.) Figure in inflation, and that equates to well over a million dollars today! At the time of Poker Chip's death in 1977, there was a survey taken among professional ropers of the day, and, by an overwhelming majority, they voted that Poker Chip was the "Greatest Roping Horse" ever lived. As a matter of fact, Poker Chip is one of only a few horses having the great honor of being buried in Oklahoma City at the National Cowboy & Western Heritage Museum.

During the early 1960s and through 1981, a total of seventeen years, Dale was president of the Professional Rodeo Cowboys Association or the "RCA" as it was known back then. With Dale at the helm, he brought the RCA into a new era. It has been said that Dale put the "P" or "Professional" into the PRCA. He was a big factor in getting the NFR moved to its longtime home in Oklahoma City (where prize money purses grew considerably). He helped increase the budget of the finals from $150,000 to over $1,000,000 during the years he was chairman of the NFR Commission. He was also a driving force in the beginning of the Pro Rodeo Cowboys Hall of Fame located in Colorado Springs, Colorado, which is now visited by hundreds of thousands of visitors each year.

He was also instrumental in getting numerous national sponsors to sponsor the sport of professional rodeo. Dale was sometimes controversial, but he always had the sports' best interest in mind. Although trying out new ideas didn't always set well, they usually worked out for the better. He took the PRCA to new heights.

From the '70s through the time of this writing, Dale has also been actively involved in the sport of quarter horse racing. Each year, people flock to Dale's ranch in Stanfield looking for that "perfect prospect." Dale has owned some of the finest racing horses in the world - household names in the industry like Late To Bed, Queen For Cash, Topless Chick, Shake It To Um, Baby Hold On, Prince Of Cash, Sign John Doe and Sign, It Super to name a few. In 1996, Sign it Super was a world-champion distance running horse at the 870-yard mark. So not only had Dale "won the world" rodeoing, but now he had won it in horse racing as well.

Besides the fact that Dale raises some fine racing horses, people also come to his ranch each year hunting for that "perfect roping horse prospect." After all, the man who once owned "The Greatest Roping Horse of All Time" ought to know a little about roping horses! You can go to ropings and rodeos all across the country and find horses that came from Dale's ranch. Just look for that famous "Johnny O" brand on their left hips.

Now, as if Dale wasn't busy enough with all of the things mentioned thus far, he also is known throughout the state of Arizona as a fine rancher. He's owned several well-known ranches in the past, including the Diamond Bar, the Lincoln Ranch, the Flying X, and the Arivaca Ranch. He was known for taking care of the land, taking care of the people working for him, and his animals, all while producing fine beef. Some of the best cowhands in the state have been in his employ at one time or another.

Dale's list of accomplishments goes on and on. We have only touched a few highlights here. You may wonder if the rest of the world took notice of Dale Smith's accomplishments like the fine people of Arizona have. Well, of course, they have. I'd bet you've heard of the National Cowboy & Western Heritage Museum Hall of Fame in Oklahoma City. Sure, most everybody has. Roy Rogers, John Wayne, Will Rogers, Gene Autry, and General George Custer are just a few of the people who have a place in the hall of fame. Guess what? Right there alongside of America's greatest cowboys, from all walks of life, is Dale Smith of Arizona. He was inducted into the hall of fame in 1996.

There is also an award named after the late great cowboy and actor, Ben Johnson. This award is given out each year to notable rodeo personnel. Dale was the recipient of the Ben Johnson Award in 2000. He is also in the Pro Rodeo Cowboy Hall Of Fame in Colorado Springs, Colorado. There is a statue of Dale and Poker Chip in "The Garden" there. Dale's list of awards is quite lengthy.

Dale Smith has spent his whole life setting goals and accomplishing them, getting what he went after. Now a lot of people who have this fame and stature might be unapproachable, aloof, or just downright stuck-up. But you can ask anyone who knows Dale - they will tell you he is just as likely to visit for hours with "Joe Blow" from down the street as he is with well-known, well-to-do famous people.

The first time I met Dale was in 1997, right after I bought my first place in the Stanfield area. No, I didn't first meet him here in Stanfield. Of all places; I met him at the Phoenix airport. I was going to catch a plane, and Dale was waiting to pick someone up. I was walking through the airport and was wearing a trophy jacket from roping. Well this old fellow just walked right up to me and said, "Hi, I'm Dale Smith. What's your name? I see that you rope!" Well, of course I knew who he was. Every young cowboy, who ropes and dreams of rodeos, had heard all about Dale Smith and the famous Poker Chip.

For the next hour or so we sat and visited until I almost missed my plane. I felt like we were long-lost friends when we parted ways. He

Dale and Marty Smith with a few of Dale's trophies. *Photo by Jim Olson*

invited me to "come and see him any ole time" and was delighted to hear we'd be neighbors. But that's just the way Dale is: He's a friend to all and has time to visit with everyone. The old Will Rogers saying comes to mind: "A stranger is just a friend that I haven't met yet." That could also apply to Dale Smith.

Dale is just as likely to have a world champion cowboy call to see how he's doing as he is to be outside visiting with locals, looking at horses. He still is, and always will be, that charismatic fellow who charmed the world while at the same time accomplishing his goals and dreams. Dale Smith is a "people person."

Darnell family

Clarence "Casey" Darnell

Natural Born Horseman

Raised on a large ranch in the San Bernardino Valley, an area encompassing the "boot heel" of New Mexico and the very southeastern portion of Arizona, Casey Darnell was born a cowboy in 1917. This area is well-known for its good "cowboy" ranching families. It was the haunt of Geronimo and Cochise before that. Tough characters have been molded from the clay of this area for a very long time.

The talented Casey was a Professional Rodeo Cowboy Association (PRCA) gold card member; inducted into the American Quarter Horse Association (AQHA) Hall of Fame; an honorary vice president of the AQHA; past president of the New Mexico Horse breeders association and New Mexico Quarter Horse Racing Association; and an AQHA director and judge for 21 years. He trained and showed a world champion performance horse, flew 27 bombing missions over Germany during WWII, and the list goes on. What most folk will tell you about Casey Darnell first off, however, is, "He had a way with horses."

Daughter, Emily Darnell Nunez, had this to say about her father, "When my dad would walk into the barn, every horse in the place would stick their head out over the stall gate as if they were greeting him. He'd then proceed to visit each one, talking to them like they were his kids. Some he praised. Others got a pep talk. But each one couldn't wait to get a visit from him. It's as if he had a special connection to them."

Casey went through several transitions throughout his fabled career as a horseman. He started off in the ranching world where, as a kid, he was horseback more often than not. Then came rodeo where he became known as a top contender. Next he moved into reining and show horses where he gained even more notoriety, and, in the latter stage of his life, horse racing became king. All these genres involve horses, but they are distinctly different. Few excel at more than one of these during a lifetime. Casey was gifted in the horse department.

Brother, Fred Darnell, of Animas, New Mexico, once wrote, "Ounce for ounce—pound for pound—Clarence Ellsworth Darnell was the best hand I've ever seen. He didn't give a darn if a horse bucked, ran off, or fell over backward; he kept on grinning and making a hand."

As a rodeo competitor, Casey was a top hand. He excelled in the roping and bull dogging events. For many years he traveled the West, making countless friends along the way. He even placed at the "Daddy" of 'em all, Cheyenne, Wyoming! Although not a big man physically, he overcame physical limitations with horsemanship skills - and cowboy grit. He was a long-time member of the PRCA, eventually becoming a lifetime gold card member.

Casey spent many years in the horse show world as well. He trained and showed about all classes and types of horses, including reining. In 1957, he had a world-champion performance horse named Skippity Scoot. Along the way, he transitioned from being a competitor to that of a highly sought-after judge. While spending 21 years as an official AQHA judge, Casey was known for being impartial to possible outside influences around the shows. He didn't care if you were a world champion or a beginner; he called it how he saw it on *that day*.

Once, when asked by a champion, who was used to winning, "Why didn't we [the contestant and horse] win?" Casey replied, "Well now, you did not have the best horse out there today." He did not sugarcoat things, but he had a way of putting it that made you like it ... never malicious and still grinning.

In the early 1960s, Casey was introduced to horse racing, and it became a passion of his thereafter. During a family visit with wife Blair's kinfolk in the east, they stopped at a thoroughbred farm in Kentucky. Casey was hooked. He bought his first thoroughbred on the spot. He was a regular in Southwestern racing circles from then on. A horse Casey trained and raced at Santa Fe Downs even wound up running in the Kentucky Derby. Son Cliff Darnell, who is also a trainer, qualified the horse for the Derby where it wound up running ninth out of a field of nineteen. Casey was pleased with his involvement.

Judge Casey, ever watchful. Photo courtesy of Darnell family

Casey once said, "I love what I do. I love training horses." He went on to give this advice, "You have to do the little things well."

Casey was well known - a legend you might say - in the New Mexico horseracing world, but his connections reached far beyond the racetrack. Casey knew everybody. Well, maybe not *everybody*, but he had a lot of influence and was well renown.

Daughter Mary Darnell said, "He never felt out of place, whether he was in New York City or Apache, Arizona ... it was all the same to him. My mom would take him to various functions around the world, and he would dress in his tux, if required, but always had his boots and hat added to the ensemble ... and people loved him wherever he went."

Daughter Emily recalls being at an event in Tingly Coliseum in Albuquerque, sitting with her dad. "The then governor of the state of New Mexico, Bruce King, stopped to shake hands and visit with my dad as if he was somebody important." She recalls thinking, "Wow, my dad must know everybody!" Casey made friends easily and had them all across the country.

Casey and wife Blair were also active in youth activities. Not only did they teach their own children to become involved in equine activities, but they introduced many other youths to the horse world as well. This often made the difference in a youth's life, helping them choose between a good path and bad. They loved the 4H program and were involved as leaders. But more than that, they did simple things, such as taking kids on trail rides and pack trips into the mountains. They became such authorities on the subject of training youths with horses that they were featured in a *Western Horseman* article, giving detailed advice on the matter. In part, Casey had this to say, "Riding, to most parents, is a way to get a kid past a certain stage ... there are some kids that will go on with it ... these mature boys and girls will get great satisfaction out of being able to make a horse do what they want him to do."

Casey got his nickname while still a youth on the family ranch. Although his first name was Clarence, he was dubbed Casey because he could drive a bulldozer, cleaning dirt tanks, and whatnot so well that he was named in honor of the legendary railroad engineer, Casey Jones.

Daughter Mary also tells us of another amazing feat accomplished by Casey, which had nothing to do with horses. It involved his time in the army during WWII. Before being drafted, Casey was simply a working cowboy. He listed "cowpuncher" as his occupation on military papers. But, ironically, within about sixty days of joining the military he was flying a B-26 bomber over Germany. Talk about being thrown into something in a hurry! Casey wound up flying twenty-seven missions during the war - quite different from the "cow punching" job he had right before. After the war, however, Casey did not talk much about his time there, and he never showed an interest in flying again, keeping to his beloved horses instead.

A former Arizona state legislator, Ralph Cowan, wrote a letter of recommendation for Casey. In part it reads, "He is loyal, honest, and above board at all times and can be relied upon to do his best in whatever he may be called upon to do."

Daughter Mary said, "He always told me do what you love, work at it every day, and the rest will fall into place."

Clarence "Casey" Darnell died in 2001, but his legendary status in the horse world lives on. Words from his tombstone pretty much sum it up - "Well Done."

Casey once said, "Get in the hunt. Believe in yourself. Work hard. Watch and listen. Don't forget to laugh. Plan for the future. Go after your dream."

Courtesy of Wayne Brooks (with permission)

Wayne Brooks

Rodeo Announcer Extraordinaire

Thousands watch the Wrangler National Finals Rodeo (NFR) every year in December. Folks sit mesmerized as it plays out under the bright lights of Las Vegas, Nevada, at the Thomas and Mack Arena. They are treated to a spectacular show, only getting bigger and better each year.

For many, many years Bob Tallman and Boyd Polhamus have been the mainstay live announcers at the NFR. Once in a while, however, there is an additional announcer working the performances alongside the veterans. Announcing at the NFR could be likened to Thom Brennaman calling the action at the World Series or John Madden commentating at the Super Bowl. It's a big deal.

Wayne Brooks is one of the fortunate few who have the distinct privilege of announcing the live action at the NFR there beside Bob and Boyd.

Wayne's rise to announcer stardom is an interesting story. You may not believe it, but Wayne's first gig as an announcer came purely by accident. He was entered in the bareback riding event at a rodeo at Estrella Park located southwest of the Phoenix, Arizona area. It just so happens the announcer who was hired to MC that particular rodeo was a no-show. So the stock contractor's wife was frantically searching around for someone to take his place announcing for the day.

She asked around, inquiring if anyone had any prior experience announcing, listening to people talk with each other as she moved about the participants. When she walked by and heard Wayne talking with his buddies, she went up to him and asked him to announce the rodeo, as he seemed to have the voice for it.

Wayne's first reaction was, "No way," but after some coaxing he reluctantly agreed. The contractor liked his voice and urged him to announce future performances. The two men made a deal. Wayne would announce the rodeos in exchange for free bareback riding practice on the contractor's horses. Little did either of them know at the time, but Wayne would go on to become one of the top announcers in all of professional rodeo and rise to superstar status in the rodeo announcing field.

Wayne Brooks came from humble beginnings, raised in the West as the son of a man who spent most of his career in the western wear and real estate businesses. Most of Wayne's childhood upbringing occurred in Wyoming, where his family has deep ranching roots that trace back to when his great grandfather settled on a ranch near Manville, Wyoming. Wayne's great grandfather was a member of the original Cattleman's Association in Wyoming and is said to have taken part in the now famous Johnson County War of the late 1800s. That original family ranch is still in Wayne's family. One of Wayne's uncles ranches there today.

When he was a senior in high school, Wayne's family moved to Yuma, Arizona, to run a western wear store there. He spent the next several years in Arizona and worked at everything from being a custom hat maker to a concrete finisher while enjoying his favorite pastime of rodeoing. It was during this time that he met and fell in love with Melanie Clark, who was fresh out of Texas and had moved to the Phoenix area to work in the banking business. They met at a rodeo dance in Scottsdale.

The happy couple now has two beautiful daughters and an outgoing young son. As it turned out, their son was born on that fateful day of 9-11-01. While the entire world was watching the tragedy of the Twin Towers coming down, the Brooks family was watching the miracle of life happen. Wayne is very proud of his family and says family is first and foremost in his life.

Since its humble beginning, Wayne's rodeo announcing career has added an impressive list of notable accomplishments. It was a long trail to climb from the Estella Park rodeo grounds in the early 1990s to the NFR, but Wayne persevered by hard work and dedication (not to mention a natural talent for announcing rodeos).

Announcer, Wayne Brooks, promo picture. Photo by Kay Levie, courtesy of Wayne Brooks.

Besides being chosen to announce performances at the NFR, he has announced the National Finals Steer Roping, the Dodge National Circuit Finals, the Canadian Finals Rodeo, and the "Tour" Finale's Rodeo several times. Add that to seven of the twelve different Circuit Finals, the Indian National Finals, the College Finals, Canada's Calgary Stampede, California's Salinas Rodeo, the Reno Rodeo, Austin's Star of Texas Rodeo, Colorado's Greeley Stampede, Tucson's Fiesta de los Vaqueros, and ... the list goes on. It is plain to see he has had a stellar rodeo announcing career, and those statistics keep adding up each year!

Wayne not only brings a great-sounding voice to the microphone, but he also brings knowledge of the events only a true cowboy and rodeo competitor can bring. You can detect Wayne's long Western heritage in each and every performance he announces. Because of that, his peers chose him as the 2005 Professional Rodeo Announcer of the Year! What a great honor and it speaks volumes regarding Wayne's talent.

When asked about any "announcing" influences he had along the way, Wayne is quick to mention his old friend and local Arizona announcer, Dan Fowlie, who helped him out tremendously during those first several performances back at the Estrella Park Rodeo Arena. He says Dan is witty and quick on his feet - just plain entertaining to listen to. (If you have ever heard Dan Fowlie at work, you would probably agree wholeheartedly with that statement.) Wayne also listens to the great announcers on a regular basis and mentions Randy Corley, Hadley Barrett, Bob Tallman, and Boyd Polhamus, among others, as people he likes to listen to and tries to pick up pointers from.

Wayne loves to be around the great people of rodeo. He is convinced his kids are more socially advanced from spending their summers on the road with him, interacting with the rodeo crowd. June, July, and August of each year are like a big ole family vacation to the Brooks family as they travel to places like Calgary, Reno, and the Oregon Coast while Wayne announces.

Wayne very much enjoys team roping, and he dabbles in real estate development while at home near Lampasas, Texas. However, he is content with his rodeo announcing career for now. He hopes to have several more good years at the level he now enjoys. Someday he says he hopes to get in a little more roping time when things slow down a bit.

Wayne Brooks feels like he is the luckiest man in the world by getting to do something he loves to do for a living, meeting such great people as he travels across the country. and being blessed with such a wonderful, supportive family.

Wayne Brooks is living proof that fate can intervene and lead you in exciting new directions if just let it. If he had not taken that leap of faith, Wayne might still be a concrete finisher today. Follow your dreams - look where it took Wayne!

Zivic family photo

William Zivic

He Knew "The King" … and "The Duke"

In the summer of 2006, I wrote about an upcoming charity event happening in our area. In one of the articles, I misstated the date of John Wayne's birth, which happens to be May 26, 1907. I thought the error might go unnoticed, but, after the print date, one William T. (Bill) Zivic immediately contacted me.

Mr. Zivic informed me I had gotten John Wayne's birthday wrong, and he oughta know, because he spent a lot of time with "Duke" in Tucson. This information interested me, so over the next several months, I had the pleasure to visit Zivic on several occasions and learn more about this accomplished gentleman.

William T. Zivic is first and foremost a Western artist. He has completed an estimated 30,000 paintings throughout his life and a number of sculptures. A freelance artist since 1967, he was the owner and operator of Zivic Art Studio in the Tucson Mall for twenty years. He had a shop in Trail Dust Town for three years (until it burned in 1971) and had paintings displayed for sale in bank lobbies, hotels, cafés, steak houses, art stores, and over the Internet. Recognized in "Who's Who in American Art," "Who's Who in the West," "Who's Who in America," and "Who's Who in the World," he has literally sold his artwork worldwide.

Born in 1930 in Ironwood, Michigan, he has worked at an array of jobs, including stints as an underground miner, merchant seaman, machinist, oil pipeline survey crewman, and detective with the Tucson

Police Department. But drawing has always been his true calling. Zivic is a self-taught artist who always knew he had "a knack for drawing." Way back in elementary school, people were making a big deal over his drawings.

It was also in the cards for Zivic to meet and befriend numerous famous people throughout his lifetime. As far back as the early 1950s, when he was in the U.S. Army during the Korean War, and later in Germany, he had the occasion to come into contact with notables. One of the greatest all-around cowboys of all time, Jim Shoulders was in the Army with him, as was "The King," Elvis Presley (at different times). The King and Bill had pictures made together while in Germany, and he says they visited quite a bit, becoming friends during that time.

During the 1960s, Bill moved to Tucson to work as a detective for the Tucson Police Department. In the line of duty, he was preforming an investigation, which took him out to Old Tucson Studios. It was 1964, and John Wayne was filming *El Dorado*. Consequently, Detective Zivic had the opportunity to meet Duke.

Zivic was already doing artwork on the side to supplement his police income, and John Wayne liked what he saw. Duke eventually became a collector of Zivic's art. He and Duke became friends; the two men visited on numerous occasions throughout the years when Wayne was in the Tucson area.

One day while the two were having a bite to eat, Bill Zivic looks at John Wayne and tells him, "This is the best day of my life. It can't go anywhere but downhill from here." John Wayne asked him what he meant by that, and Zivic told him, "Well, I'm sitting here having lunch with John Wayne, an American legend, and I just don't see how it could ever get any better." Duke just laughed and humbly told him that wasn't true - he really wasn't any different than anyone else.

Bill Zivic's artwork opened the door for him to meet numerous others whose names you'd recognize. Some would even say that Zivic became quite famous himself. During the 1960s and 1970s, while he was cranking out Western paintings left and right, many movies were filmed in and around the Tucson area. It seems that word got out among the movie crowd about this artist who could draw Western

"The King" and Bill Zivic in uniform. *Photo courtesy of Zivic family*

scenes, portraits, and caricatures like nobody's business.

In addition to Wayne, the artist visited with the likes of James Garner, Ben Johnson, Roy Rogers, James Caan, and Bob Hope, to name a few. He sold artwork to many of the actors he met. His artwork has graced the cover of books, the Toyota Corporate Headquarters in Japan, the Roy Rogers Museum, and, of course, John Wayne's home. His art hangs in the Rodeo Cowboy Hall of Fame and around the world.

One thing he's proud of is that he is an artist of "the people," meaning his artwork is affordable enough for most anyone to enjoy. He thinks that everyone should be able to enjoy original art, not just the rich. "My artwork sells to dishwashers and to celebrities," Zivic says proudly.

The fact that he has a knack for drawing sure helps in this department. You see, he might work on as many as ten to fifteen different paintings at a time, all in various stages of completion and drying. A lot of artist couldn't do that. It's because of the ease with which the paintings come to him that has enabled him to complete so many paintings.

That's also what has kept his artwork affordable, selling anywhere from $10 to $5,000. Even in "semi-retirement" at over eighty, he is still cranking out paintings, although not at the same pace as years before when he was supporting a growing family through art sales. Still sold over the Internet, as well in several other outlets, you can collect this artist's work just like Duke and many other famous people have.

Mr. Zivic is an interesting gentleman to visit with, and he has a great sense of humor. If you ever get the chance to meet the man who knew The King…and The Duke, you will be in for a good time.

William T. Zivic is a humble man, but a great human being. Here is a man who put his natural, God-given talents to work and, because of it, became such an accomplished Western artist!

Courtesy of Larkin family

Pat Larkin

The Man Behind the Scenes

Have you ever watched a movie or a show and wondered, "How'd they do that?" I have. More specifically, when I watch a western movie (my favorite kind of course), I think of little things like, "Wow, I wonder who trained that horse to fall on cue?" Or maybe, "How did they get that horse to rear, count, sit down, act drunk," or whatever the case may be? Who owns that herd of cattle they are trailing? Where did they get that cool wagon? Where did they find that old pickup truck? All of these things are of interest to me, so I did a little research and found a man who could answer my questions.

Pat Larkin was born in Kansas in 1936, and now, more than a few years later, he is still going strong. From the time Pat was just a little guy, he knew what he really wanted out of life was to be a cowboy. At the age of about ten, Pat went to live with his granddad on his ranch in rural Kansas. Pat's parents lived in town and were in the saloon business, but Pat was more interested in being out in the country with Grandpa. So he loaded up his things and went out to live on granddad's ranch, only visiting his parents every once in a while. Pat's parents just knew that he craved the ranch life more than town life, and it seemed a better place for him anyway.

During his formative years on the ranch, Pat learned to drive teams of horses that were hooked to a plow or a wagon. Much of the farming and ranching back in those days was still done with horses and mules, because a good part of the rural community couldn't afford tractors.

He learned a lot about ranch animals during that time with horses being his favorite. As Pat grew up, his passion for horses and ranch life turned into a passion for rodeo. In his younger days, he worked just about every rodeo event you could enter (as was common back then). When Pat wasn't working, rodeoing, or going to school, a favorite pastime was combing the countryside looking for adventure a-horseback. He spent a lot of time with the horses, which has since turned into a lifelong connection with them.

One day, while still in high school, Pat was dealing blackjack at his dad's saloon (that's another story) and something happened that opened up a whole new world of possibilities. There happened to be a movie crew in town, which was shooting some scenes for a western movie. A couple of guys from the movie crew were in the bar, and they were having a conversation about difficulties with this certain scene. The scene involved jumping a horse off of a cliff and into the river below. The horse needed to be in a full gallop when he hit the edge of the cliff, and then, once in the water, the horse and its rider had to swim to the other bank.

A relative of Pat's overheard this conversation. He then approached the movie crew guys and pointed them in Pat's direction. They were told Pat did stuff like that just for fun and adventure. Much to the relief of the movie crew, Pat agreed to meet them on location the next morning and perform the stunt. Everything went off as planned. The movie crew got their shot, and Pat couldn't believe that he had actually gotten paid for doing something so fun and easy. He had done that very thing before and probably would have performed for free - if they had just asked.

From that humble introduction into the world of making movies, Pat has since grown into a living legend. Although not his first career choice (which would have been rodeo), the movie business kept getting into his path over and over again. It seems he was destined to be in movie production in some form or another.

He has performed numerous jobs behind the scenes while making a movie, commercial, or TV show. He has been stuntman and stunt coordinator; provided transportation and props, such as wagons and, of course, animals. As a matter of fact, Pat says, "There were times I

One of Pat's rearing horses at work. *Photo by Pat Larkin*

had up to five different things going on at five different sets, simultaneously!" Now that's busy.

Pat is probably best-known for the animals he has provided over the years, especially stunt horses. He has owned some of the most famous stunt/trick horses in show business. Ace and Spiffy are two of the top horses that come to mind, but they are not the only ones. He has also had the good fortune of being able to learn from and work with some of the world's best animal trainers. During his long and prestigious career in the movie business, he has trained horses to rear (with and without a rider), fall, count, indicate "yes" and "no," pull the saddle blanket off, kneel, and numerous other tricks. Pat also had cattle that would do a lot of those same tricks. I can just about guarantee that you have seen some of Pat's animals and props at work while watching a movie.

It is no surprise Pat has some interesting stories to tell from over the years.

For example, most people have seen (or at least heard of) the movie *Braveheart*, which was directed by Mel Gibson who also starred in the movie. Movie buffs may also know that *Braveheart* was filmed in Ireland and Scotland, but what most movie buffs don't know was some of the best horse action scenes in that movie were actually filmed just outside of Benson, Arizona. Furthermore; the horses that rear right into the camera during the battle scenes belonged to none other than Pat Larkin.

It all started like this: Pat gets a call from a stunt coordinator he knew, and the guy asks him, "Can you be in Benson in a couple days and bring as many rearing horses as you can?" So Pat showed up in Benson with a trailer load of horses, but still didn't know what he was going to be working on. After everyone was briefed and prepared for the scene, the director flew in by helicopter. None other than Mel Gibson stepped out, and then he proceeds to tell Pat that they were having trouble getting what he wanted out of the stunt horses in Ireland for this movie. Apparently, this field near Benson could pass for the background, and now he needed some "real" horses and stuntmen to give him the shot he was looking for.

The rest is on film, and, if you watch that movie and see where the horses look like they are rearing right on top of the camera, well, those are Pat's horses. He chuckles when he recalls the cameramen "abandoning ship" and leaving their cameras unattended when the horses reared right over them. "There were tracks all around those cameras," recalls Pat, "but there wasn't one single scratch on them from any of my animals."

Another well-known western movie photo was that of Will Smith on the cover of *Vanity Fair* as he did the promotion for *Wild Wild West*. If you have ever seen the promotional trailer for *Wild Wild West* or the aforementioned cover shot, then you've seen Pat's horse, Ace. He was

Will Smith on Pat's horse "Ace."
Provided by Pat Larkin

the one Smith was riding. Pat says that when they shot those promotional scenes it was very cold outside. So while Will and the camera crew were at work, Pat sat inside a warm Cadillac Escalade with Will's wife, Jada Pinkett Smith, and munched on chocolate chip cookies with her.

"Both Will and Jada were very nice people and easy to be around," notes Pat.

But being around stars and the movie life is nothing new to Pat. After practically a lifetime of working around the business, nothing surprises him. He says it's been a long time since he felt "starstruck." Some of the sets on which Pat has worked include *How the West was Won*, *Cat Ballou*, *True Grit*, *Tombstone*, and hundreds of others that it would take too long to mention. He estimates he has worked on about 200 movies and over 200 commercials … so far.

Even in his twilight years, Pat has not slowed down much. He still is working on movies, television, commercials, and shows under his own company banner of Arizona Stunt Specialists. Pat also has some of his own scripts, and maybe someday we will get to watch an original Pat Larkin screenplay. Along with that, he provides live stunts and entertainment for Wild West re-enactments and other events.

For relaxation and as part of their business enterprise, Pat and his family are involved in racing. He has raced numerous motorcycles and boats over the years, receiving many awards along the way. Now, Pat's grandson is keeping the family traditions alive by competing in novice racing classes. The daredevil is in the family's gene pool, I guess.

After fifty years, Pat is still married to the same lady and is still the same ol' down-to-earth cowboy he started off as. For those of us who like to watch TV and western movies, we should thank the efforts of men such as Pat for providing the entertainment "behind the scenes."

Pat Larkin is a great cowboy ambassador for the Western way of life and has a knack for letting it shine through on screen. He is proof you can remain close to your roots while maintaining a high-profile career.

Phelps family photo

Pete Phelps

Not Just Another Cowboy

If there is a man in the last half of the twentieth century you could point out as an exemplary cowboy/cattleman/horseman, that man could very well be Pete Phelps. Not only is Pete a first-rate cowboy, whether with a cow or a horse, but he is also a very likable human being. Even though Pete is now over eighty, it hasn't slowed his mind down any. Pete can tell you stories of cowboying, horses, people, and events that happened over the last fifty-plus years just like they happened yesterday.

Pete has plenty of stories to tell about the cowboy world. He is well-respected and has numerous major accomplishments. The events of his lifetime are enjoyable to hear about, and he has a contagious laugh that makes visiting with him just plain ol' fun—not only fun, but a great history lesson of the cowboy lifestyle as well. Even when just a young boy, he knew all he wanted to do in life was be a cowboy.

Pete Phelps was raised on an Iowa farm along with his eight brothers and sisters. However, he knew at an early age, farming didn't fit into his lifestyle expectations. While growing up, he liked to read stockman publications, especially ones about big ranches and horse people. One man that was well-known at the time and received a lot of notoriety was a fellow by the name of Dan Casement. Dan had a ranch in Kansas and was also big in the Fledgling Organization of the American Quarter Horse Association (AQHA).

In 1949, at the age of twenty-two, Pete Phelps left Iowa and went to Kansas in search of Dan Casement. He found out where Casement lived and showed up on his front porch, telling him, "I am Pete Phelps and I want to be a cowboy. Do you have any work for me?" Well, the then eighty-year-old Casement must have been impressed with young Pete, because he let him in and visited with him for three hours.

Casement then picked up the telephone, called his friend and neighbor Orville Burtis, told him he had a young man here who needed a job, and was sending him over in the morning - and that he should hire Pete! Burtis was another one of the founding members of the AQHA and the organization's sixth president.

During the next several years, Pete worked off and on for both Burtis and Casement. And that's how an Iowa farm boy got his start being a cowboy. He learned right off from some of the best and most-respected ranchers and horsemen in the country.

It was during this period Pete also met Richard and Helen Nelson, who were the owners of the Columbian Hog & Cattle Powder Co. of Kansas City, Missouri - one of the first animal supplement companies in the Midwest. The Nelsons had many other ventures as well, including several ranches. Pete had come highly recommended to the Nelsons as someone who could run one of their ranches, so they asked him to come and look at their Nebraska place, as they needed a new foreman there.

When Pete showed up at the ranch, the first thing he noticed was there were two big bulldozers in the shed. When asked what they were used for, Pete was told they were for pushin' snow. The next thing Pete noticed about the ranch was that there seemed to be an awful lot of haying to do. Well, that did it. Pete told the Nelsons he couldn't work for them 'cause he couldn't picture himself putting up hay all summer and then pushin' snow and feeding hay all winter!

Not to be deterred, a couple of months later the Nelsons invited Pete out to look at their Arizona ranch. The man working there had been a personal aide to a famous general during World War II, they told Pete with a laugh, but he was not much of a ranch manager.

The first time Pete drove through the gate at the Nelson's Santa Margarita Ranch in Southern Arizona, he felt like he had come home.

It was 1956, and Pete was in his prime at twenty-nine years of age. He spent the next twenty-eight years working for the Nelsons and running the Santa Margarita Ranch. He says he felt like he had "come into his own" by getting to run the Arizona ranch, surrounded by extraordinary cowboys.

This picture is a "Shoofly" drawing of Pete. Photo by Jim Olson

One of the first things Pete noticed about ranching in Arizona: It was nothing like ranching anywhere else. The ranch in Arizona, which had the best cattle and best range at that time, happened to be the Buenos Aires Ranch - right next to the Santa Margarita Ranch. Pete immediately became acquainted with Chofo Ariza, who ran the Buenos Aires Ranch. He asked Chofo lots of questions and started doing stuff just like they did on the Buenos Aires.

Times being what they were, not many people back in those days would have asked a "Mexican" for advice, but Pete didn't look at it that way. He looked at it like he was getting advice from one of the best cattlemen in the country. Well, Pete must have learned real well, because he went on to receive an award for Range Manager of the Year in 1967.

Early on, Pete discovered he had an "unwanted partner." You see, he was never married, didn't have any dependents, didn't have any expenses, and was making pretty good wages as the manager of the Santa Margarita. Pete says his partner became "the IRS."

"The worst part of it was," Pete laughs, "I was doing all of the work, and the IRS was getting half of the money." It was then Pete decided he needed to get into a business that would have some tax write-offs.

His first choice was the horse business. It seemed a natural fit, as he worked a-horseback most every day anyhow. Pete started out with three mares. The Nelsons decided they wanted to partner up with Pete in his new venture, so they all started raising horses on the Santa Margarita.

Something a bit unusual was all of the horses were to remain in Pete's name. You see, the Nelsons traveled a lot and each time a horse was bought or sold, it would be impractical to track down the Nelsons for their signatures on the bill of sale or transfer papers. Consequently, it was decided that all of the horses would remain in Pete's name, which speaks volumes about the faith Pete's employers had in him.

During his years at the Santa Margarita, he raised, raced, showed, trained, bought, and sold hundreds of horses. As a matter of fact, he became one of the best-known owners of racehorses on the Arizona racing circuit. Pete was even a founding member and six-time president of the Arizona Quarter Horse Racing Association (AQRA). He was known far and wide in the horse business and had a very respectable reputation.

Another venture Pete had during his time at the Santa Margarita was that of a judge at cattle shows. During about a ten-year period, Pete judged show cattle at most of the major stock shows around the country. He became highly sought-after and judged from Hawaii, to the Cow Palace at San Francisco, to the National Western Stock Show at Denver. Pete had become so in demand that he was getting called out more and more. It was starting to cut into his ranch work. Well, Pete wouldn't have any of that, and even though the Nelsons didn't mind him being gone, he called the Hereford Association one day and told them to take his name off of the list. He had a drought going on at the ranch, and his duties there were more important to him.

Ranching, judging show cattle, and the horse business weren't the only places Pete was in the spotlight. Back then, there was a young artist named Bob Shufelt, who came out to the Santa Margarita and wanted to take pictures of the men in action. Pete told him it was okay, just as long as he didn't get in the way, and didn't ask the cowboys to stop what they were doing and "pose." It was agreed, and the young artist went about taking pictures of the ranch and the cowboys. This artist made a couple of trips to the ranch and drew several pictures based on the photos taken.

That young fellow later became well-known as none other than "Shoo Fly." Shoo Fly even sent a drawing of Pete to President Reagan back when Reagan was in the White House. President Regan loved Pete's warm smiling face on the drawing and hung it up in the White House. Today, that drawing is in the Ronald Reagan Library. Not only was Pete the subject of many Shoo Fly drawings, but he also was featured in a print ad for the Arizona Feed Company. Pete was also featured in a Busch Beer commercial that ran for about ten years. (Pete says the beer commercial paid handsomely over the years.)

Here we have a man who is a well-respected cattleman, horseman, and cattle judge; appeared in a TV commercial and a print ad for a feed company; and was the subject of several Shoo Fly drawings (including one at the White House), but that's not all. Pete (as I mentioned) won Range Manager of the Year; was six-time president of the AQRA; and on the boards of the Arizona Cattle Growers Association, the Southern Arizona Cattleman's Protective Association, and the local school at Sasabe; and on and on.

In spite of all those other accomplishments, Pete is probably best-known overall as the man who stood the great stud Zircon. After the Nelsons sold the Santa Margarita Ranch in 1984, Pete got wholeheartedly into the horse business.

In 1987, he put together a few investors, and headed off to the racehorse sale at Ruidoso, New Mexico, to try and purchase the

Pete at corrals on Santa Margarita Ranch.
Photo courtesy of Phelps family

stud horse Zircon. Pete managed to get Zircon for $40,000, and, within one week, was offered $65,000 for him. He turned down the offer, and over the next eighteen years, Pete stood Zircon at his place near Eloy, Arizona. It's a good thing Pete turned down that initial $25,000 profit on Zircon, as the stud turned out to be Pete's bread and butter for nearly the next two decades. Zircon's descendants are scattered all over the country, and several of them have become famous in their own right. The great stud still lives at Pete's place near Eloy and will finish out the remainder of his time there grazing in green pastures.

Pete says his life has been a string of lucky events that led from one successful venture to the next. Things like going to work at his first ranch job for one of the most reputable ranchers in the country and getting Zircon bought for $40,000 when there was a man willing to pay $65,000 who just couldn't get to the sale that day are examples he mentions. A lot of successful people may say they are just lucky. I even know a lot of other people who look upon successful people as folks who just got lucky. But it seems to me that those who work the hardest, study on it the most, and try the hardest always seem to be the lucky ones.

Pete has led storybook life. So, it's no surprise that, at eighty, when you figure Pete Phelps could just be resting his weary bones, he remains in the limelight. In the spring of 2007, there was a book and audio set released titled *Not Just Another Cowboy*. This book features pictures about his life, and the audio set contains direct recordings of Pete himself, telling stories about days gone by.

His regular hangout these days is a coffee shop at Eloy, Arizona. I suggest you ask one of the waitresses there to point you in the direction of Pete Phelps. Should you get the chance to sit and visit with this cowboy - a living history book - you better be prepared for a sidesplitting, educational, and historical visit.

This is a man who always believed in going straight for the top in any field he chose. Pete Phelps is definitely a fine example of a true American cowboy who has been successful in many arenas!

Jim Olson

Pablo Osuna

Vaquero!

Anyone knowing Arizona cowboys and ropers for long has probably heard of Pablo Osuna. He is a legend among the old-timers, known as one of the best ropers, cowboys, and horsemen of the last half of the twentieth century.

He worked for some of the biggest and best outfits in Arizona, making a reputation as "top hand." He also spent many years in feedlots where his cowboy skills were much appreciated.

Outside of work, one of Pablo's favorite pastimes was roping. He was good at it. A couple of the old-time great RCA (Rodeo Cowboys Association) cowboys once commented, "We are sure glad Pablo never ventured out of Arizona much, because, if he had, things would have been a whole lot harder to win out on the rodeo trail."

Pablo was born on September 16, 1917, in the northern Mexican state of Sonora in an area known as "*La Temporal*" or "The Temporary." This means when it rained a lot, crops were planted, livestock grazed, and things were good. When it didn't rain, however, people just barely got by.

Pablo's parents knew early on he was destined to be a cowboy. When he was very little, someone showed him the basics of braiding, and from then on his mother had to hide the towels, linens, and so on from young Pablo. Whenever he got ahold of those things, he would take them apart and braid ropes and the like out of them!

His first cowboy experiences came by helping out his father at Rancho El Alamo (Alamo Ranch) just outside of Magdalena, Mexico. In addition to his cowboy chores, young Pablo attended school there.

A Harvard fellow, who turned cowboy, built Rancho El Alamo. Its headquarters resembled an ancient English castle. An old photograph taken when Pablo was about fourteen or fifteen years old appeared in the *National Geographic Magazine*, February 1955. The photo shows young Pablo kneeling, eating some grub, along with a whole crew of cowboys (including his father). The famous "Alamo castle" is in the background.

Pablo's first job on his own came when he was about fifteen, working for a neighboring ranch near Magdalena. When Pablo was sixteen, he went to work for the famous Rancho La Cananea, located just outside of Cananea, Mexico. Rancho La Cananea was a very, very large company, having mining operations in northern Mexico and ranching operations on both sides of the border. It was reported the ranch in Mexico covered 667,000 acres and at times ran as many as 24,000 head of Hereford cattle.

In 1934, when he was seventeen, something happened that changed Pablo's life and pointed him in another direction. At the urging of a couple of his friends, he went to talk to an American rancher named Bud Parker about a job. Bud had just rented Rancho Pozo Nuevo (New Well Ranch) just outside of Magdalena. Pablo went to work for him, and Bud Parker became a friend and mentor to young Pablo. Actually, Pablo came to consider him sort of like a second father.

He worked on Rancho Pozo Nuevo about five years, and then Bud brought him over to Arizona to work on his ranch north of the Benson. Bud came to appreciate the roping skills of his hired man so much that he entered Pablo in his first rodeo. He won the event. Bud wound up entering Pablo in numerous rodeos around the state after that, and the two men both supplemented their incomes nicely for it.

Another thing that Bud did for Pablo was to help him get his "papers" straight, so that he could legally live in the United States. Pablo worked for Bud until his death—a total of about fifteen or sixteen years. Bud Parker lived in the heart of a young teenager and still lives on today in the heart of a man in his nineties. Pablo speaks of his time with Bud with great emotion as he recalls things Bud did for him. Pablo says he will never forget Bud Parker.

After Bud's death, Pablo worked on several well-known ranches around Arizona, such as the Santa Margarita, The Buenos Aires, and the 3 Cs ranch. During those years, he supplemented his income by roping. He roped at most all the major ropings and rodeos in Arizona, such as the Fiesta De Los Vaqueros in Tucson and the Jaycees Rodeo in Phoenix. It was during this time he became known as one of the great Arizona ropers. Folks knew he had a good chance of winning regardless of who else happened to be entered that day. It was a good thing Pablo could make extra money with his rope, because he now had a young family to tend as well. He married the love of his life, Maria Valenzuela, in 1946, and the happy couple wound up having ten kids over the next couple of decades.

In 1960, Pablo decided to try a new venture in hopes of bettering his life and that of his family. You see, at that time it was not legal for Americans to own property in Mexico. It just so happened there was an American in the Tucson area who wanted to buy a ranch in Mexico as an investment. This man spoke to Pablo about it, and the two formed a partnership. The ranch was to be in Pablo's name, and Pablo would run it. The man put up the money for the venture, and they were to be full partners.

Pablo and his family moved back to Mexico where they ranched for the next six years or so. His family loved it there, but things were not working out financially as expected. A friend of Pablo's from the Casa Grande, Arizona area got a hold of Pablo and urged him to come to Casa Grande and help out on his ranch.

Pablo came for roundup and wound up staying. He then sent his family a letter telling them he wasn't going to go back to Mexico to ranch anymore, and, as soon as things were "tended to" down there, the family would be returning to Arizona. The family was enjoying life in Mexico, but finances were better on this side of the line.

Shortly after returning to the United States, Pablo started to work at a local feedlot. Then another feedlot in the Brawley, California area offered him more money. He and his family moved to Brawley, but, after a few months, they all were all a little homesick for Arizona.

A young Pablo and Maria Osuna.   *Photo courtesy of Osuna family*

On one of his days off, Pablo went to visit a friend at a feed yard near Maricopa, Arizona. While talking with his friend, the boss drove by and saw Pablo. Once spotted, he was offered a job immediately. It didn't take much urging for Pablo to accept, and soon the family had relocated to the Maricopa area—much to their delight. He spent the next twenty years working for the Producers and Pinal feed yards. He worked there until his retirement at age seventy in 1987. During those years, while he worked the Maricopa feed yards, the local jackpot ropings and rodeos were a little tougher for others to win thanks to his presence.

After his retirement in 1987, he couldn't sit still for very long. He wound up doing day work for ranches and odd jobs related to horses for the next several years. It was only as he approached ninety that he finally quit working so hard.

Pablo loves to recall the old days. With a faraway gleam in his eyes, he'll sit and tell stories of chasing wild cows on half-broke horses in even wilder country. As he describes the men with whom he worked, the horse he was riding, the country, the situation, it's almost as if you were there yourself, dodging mesquite limbs, jumping boulders, crashing the brush until you line out on an old wild maverick.

When you ask old-timers about Pablo Osuna, a comment you'll often hear is, "Pablo is a great horseman." He trained countless horses throughout his life as he went about his cowboy duties. It has often been said he had a special connection with them. A local veterinarian refers to him as "*El Brujo*" (loosely translated "The Wizard" or the "The Witch Doctor"). This is done good-naturedly and refers to the fact Pablo is well versed in the making of liniments, salves, and such which people have been using for centuries to cure what ails an animal. These types of cures predate what the vets use and, in a lot of cases, work as good or better.

When Pablo's daughter, Silvia, first became interested in riding with the quadrille team, she rode Pablo's horse, Johnny, in the events. The other ladies of the team were so impressed with how Johnny worked for Silvia that, within a few years, most of the quadrille team members were riding horses Pablo had trained for them. One horse Pablo likes to recall was a sorrel horse named Indio. He punched cattle and roped on Indio, but Indio was also a favorite and quite well known among the ladies of the quadrille.

Many an Arizona cowboy wound up riding a Pablo Osuna-trained horse with pride. Whether they used them in the arena or out in the open country, they could always count on the horse having a good foundation from his trainer.

Life has slowed down a bit for Pablo now that he is over ninety. However, he loves to visit and talk about cowboying, recalling the old days with great clarity and emotion. He has lived a way of life that many only read about in stories. In my opinion, there hasn't been a Hollywood screenplay done yet that would do a better job of recounting the life of a true cowboy.

Pablo lives today, however, just as he has lived his entire life: humble and down-to-earth:

"Do the very best that you can."

"Work honorably."

"You are no better than anyone else, and no one else is any better than you."

These are all words Pablo believes in and lives by. He has done so his entire life.

Pablo "*El Prieto*" Osuna—*usted es un heroe de los vaqueros.*

Pablo is an example of a man who did not let being born into poverty affect his chances at a good life. No matter where you start from in life, a down-to-earth, positive attitude, mixed with a good work ethic, can take you wherever you wish to go.

Charles Brooks

JW Brooks
The Hat Maker

One of the most recognizable symbols of the American West is the cowboy hat. While worn today for a variety of reasons, most having little to do with the original purpose, being used as a tool ushered in its existence.

The history of the cowboy hat can be traced to the 1860s. A fellow named John B. Stetson was on a hunting trip out West. As a joke, he fashioned a large brimmed hat with a high crown out of fur, wearing it during the excursion. Before long, however, it was apparent to the group that John's hat served many useful purposes, such as shade, keeping water off in a rainstorm, watering your horse, and fanning a fire.

Within a few years, John was making hats by the hundreds for people all over the West. The Mexican vaqueros of the Southwest had been using a similar hat called a *sombrero* for many years prior to that as shade, but the "Stetson" was definitely the first of its kind. It soon became known as the hat of the American cowboy.

Today, you have many choices of cowboy hats to choose from. Each hat says something unique about its wearer. Most of these, however, fall into two basic categories: factory-made hats and custom-made hats

Factory-made hats are mass-produced, come in basic sizes and styles, and are generally less expensive. Custom-made hats are made one at a time to fit the person who ordered it, styled to that person's specifications, generally thought of as being of "higher quality," and usually cost a little more - but are well worth it to the "discerning" hat wearer. One man who has become a master in the making of custom hats is none other than John W Brooks (aka JW to those who know him).

JW has been building custom hats since 1991, and learned the trade by working for reputable hat makers such as Kevin O'Farrell, Aztec Hats, Saba's Western Wear, Perryman's Western Wear, and Durango Hats. JW has been crafting custom-made hats on his own since 1998, and he's become known as one of the best in the business.

Numerous professional cowboys proudly wear his hats. Some you might know include rodeo notables such as Cody Demoss, Colter Todd, Cesar de la Cruz, Cody Hancock, Cody Demers, and Shali Lord. Famous rodeo announcers, such as Bob Tallman and Wayne Brooks (JW's brother), also wear his hats.

JW Brooks Custom Hats are even worn by entertainers such as California wildman Don "Hollywood" Yates (the bullfighter turned *American Gladiator* star who is known as "The Wolf" from *American Gladiator*) and *Cowboy U* host Rocco Wachman from the popular CMT show. Yet, JW is especially proud that hundreds of everyday cowboys, who really know and appreciate a good hat, are also satisfied customers.

If you have ever owned a JW Brooks custom-made hat, then you are truly wearing a piece of wearable art. You see JW *is* an artist. As a matter of fact, he illustrated a children's book while still only in the fourth grade. He says, "Artwork has always come naturally to me even though I didn't get any special training in the art department."

JW was the featured artist for the Phoenix Rodeo of Rodeos on three different occasions and also the Scottsdale Parada Del Sol Rodeo on a few occasions. As a matter of fact, being an artist is what led JW into the hat-making business.

While attending high school in Durango, Colorado, he entered a talent contest as a singer. JW needed a new hat for the contest and went to see custom hat-maker Kevin O'Farrell. O'Farrell liked JW's artwork and ended up trading a hat for some of his art. Both men were happy with the trade. Then O'Farrell had a hunch JW's artistic talent would work nicely in the hat-making business, so he offered JW a job. He apprenticed under O'Farrell Hats for three years, and the rest is history.

JW Brooks custom made hats. *Photo by Charles Brooks*

Besides being a talented artist, JW is a great singer as well. As I mentioned, entering a talent contest as a singer is what led to him trading art for a hat. Fast forward a few years and he became the lead singer of a country band known as Western Bred.

In 2004, he entered the *Nashville Star* talent search contest and won first place at the Arizona state level. While he did not win the national contest, it did help him launch a singing career. Western Bred has since become known as one of Arizona's top country bands, playing popular venues all over the state.

Being talented runs in the Brooks family I guess. His beautiful wife, Jody, is also very talented and does a lot of modeling and charity work. She's a member of the Cowgirls Historical Foundation, was on the board of directors for the Georgia Reining Cow Horse Association in her native state of Georgia, and has managed a horseback drill team. JW's brother is none other than popular Pro Rodeo announcer Wayne Brooks. Wayne has done quite well himself as a PRCA announcer of the year and as a Wrangler National Finals Rodeo and National Finals Steer Roping announcer. I guess, when such a talented family surrounds you, it brings out the best in you.

Even though he is gifted artistically in music and art, making a great hat is JW's passion. He says each hat he makes is made with pride and to complement its wearer. Not only does JW build your traditional cowboy hats for working cowboys, professional cowboys, and entertainers, but the truly artistic side of him surfaces in some of the hats he builds.

What I am referring to is that JW also builds hats with a little "bling" and uniqueness to them. These are fashioned after suits such as your Nudie Cohen or Manuel rhinestone-studded outfits. Hats with floral designs in contrasting colors or hats with bling are built for members of the Cowgirls Historical Foundation to go with their historical period clothing or built for people who have that wild personality about them. Many other hat makers are copying this new style, but JW was the first to do it.

Something special about each and every JW Brooks hat is each one is made for the particular person who ordered it: It is truly "custom" and says a lot about who that person is. "And if you don't like it, send it back and I will make it right until you're satisfied," says JW.

He conducts his business with true cowboy ethics that were "Western Bred" into him. JW has a long ranching background, which has historical ties to Wyoming and Colorado, even dating back to the Johnson County War of 1892.

Being a cowboy and true to his Western roots are important to him. JW Brooks Custom Hats's list of clientele now span the entire West.

JW is a man who turned a passion into a profession. The easiest thing he could have done in life would have been to work for a commercial hat manufacturer, drawing a regular paycheck and stifling his true artistic nature. Taking risks in life can pay big in the satisfaction department - it did for JW!

Jim Olson

Gary Sprague
The Singing Cowboy

One of the great western icons is that of "the singing cowboy." On your TV, not all that many years ago, you could count on being able to see a "good guy," usually in a white hat, doing what was morally right while protecting the weak and innocent. The good guy so prevalent in shows and movies back then was usually a "singing cowboy." When not fighting outlaws and protecting the innocent, he would make you feel good, entertaining you with a song.

Probably the two fellas who come to mind, when you think of those singing cowboys, are Gene Autry and Roy Rogers. There were hundreds of others, however, who were also very popular at different times. Did you know that even John Wayne himself gave it a whirl as "Singing Sandy" early in his career?

In the modern world, however, guys like Roy Rogers, Gene Autry, Hopalong Cassidy, Rex Allen, Tex Ritter, and others have largely been forgotten. What a shame. These guys were heroes on the big and small screens to a couple generations of Americans. During the peak of the singing cowboy era, which was during the 1940s and early '50s, these guys were as big as Johnny Depp, John Travolta, and Antonio Banderas are today. Well, as they say, "Gone but not forgotten."

You may be happy to know there are still singing cowboys out there, riding the trails forged by the great cowboys of the past. One such man is none other than Arizona's own singing cowboy, Gary Sprague.

When you first see him, you're immediately reminded of the silver screen cowboys, such as Autry and Rogers. Dressed in period cowboy clothing with authentic "six shooters" and guitar, and riding on his trusty horse, Dusty, Gary reminds you of those singing cowboys of yesteryear.

Not only does he look the part, but he can walk the walk, and talk the talk. He sings volumes of old-time cowboy favorites, recites cowboy poetry by the pages, and tells cowboy stories like nobody's business. Gary is very talented with a guitar, and his booming voice will keep the attention of any crowd, even in large outdoor areas.

He has become one of the most highly sought-after entertainers in Arizona when it comes to cowboy entertainment. He is so good at it; his sole source of income for the last couple of decades has been that of a cowboy entertainer, portraying the old-time singing cowboys. Thousands of tourist and locals alike witness his shows throughout the year. He is an authentic singing cowboy as there ever was. What most don't know, however, is that Gary's true calling, as an authentic cowboy entertainer, came via an unlikely journey.

Gary was born during the early 1950s in ... of all places ... upstate New York. He grew up there, the son of a carpenter. When he became an adult, he was your typical eight-to-five employee working for corporate America - an everyday Joe from the East Coast. That was what the world would have thought, at first glance anyway. But Gary knew differently.

He had always enjoyed music, playing in a band for many years. He even tried to make a living as a musician during his early twenties, but you know how life goes for most folks: get married, get a job - settle into a "normal" life. That was Gary Sprague's story until his late thirties, "just your ordinary average guy."

However, he had, as I mentioned, always loved music. He also loved animals and had spent a good deal of time around them. While growing up, Gary had thoroughly enjoyed watching his silver screen heroes, the singing cowboys and their portrayal of the great American West. So, at the age of thirty-seven, Gary had a long talk with his wife... then quit his job, "pulled up stakes," and moved to Arizona!

Talk about a change of lifestyle. One day you're an average guy from upstate New York, and the next you live in Arizona with no job and no real plan (or so some thought). Gary, however, did have a plan: to play country and western music.

That first year in Arizona, he taught himself the words and chords to ninety different songs. He worked hard at being a musician, and his first break came by being able to play nights at a famous Western steakhouse/lounge in the Scottsdale area.

As he worked hard to hone his craft and become a better and better "Western" entertainer, he wondered, "Where had all the cowboys gone?" Obviously Gene and Roy had retired long ago, but was there anyone out there like them anymore?

He talked with his colleagues about entertaining from a horse and met with resistance (not to mention a few giggles). Not one to be deterred, he borrowed a horse and sang in a parade. The people who loaned him the horse thought that, since the horse was, shall we say, not all that well-behaved, Gary would give up and forget all of this nonsense about entertaining on horseback. Yet, just the opposite happened. He loved entertaining on horseback, and, after a few times, he had the horse acting much better as well. So much better in fact, that the people now wanted the horse back to use themselves.

After that, Gary got a horse of his own, and the rest, shall we say, is history.

His act started to evolve. He loved watching his singing cowboy heroes while growing up, and he now enjoyed entertaining like those before him. One thing led to another, and, before long, he was outfitted in a big black hat, wore chaps, boots and spurs, and had a handkerchief around his neck when he went to work.

Gary started learning more and more of the old-time songs, recited poetry, and told cowboy stories. He worked hard at portraying the old-time singing cowboy. He studied Old West history for countless hours.

Hard work paid off. One thing led to another and word got around about this authentic "singing cowboy." Gary was invited to play Old West haunts like Merv Griffin's Wickenburg Inn, Greasewood Flats, The Wigwam and even The Biltmore to name a few. He is also a regular fixture in Old Town Scottsdale during the tourist season.

He has played countless corporate events and parties, and even rode out to center ice to sing the national anthem at a Phoenix Coyotes hockey game. Although Gary has been dubbed "Arizona's Singing Cowboy" for quite some time now, he has also been featured on numerous shows outside of the state, including national coverage on the BBC Channel, *Good Morning America*, a Kansas news channel, and even the nationally syndicated *Travel Café* show. He has also been featured in lots of newspaper and magazine articles around the country.

Gary Sprague has become quite a master of his craft, and that is not by chance. He continues to work diligently at what he does. Not only does he work hard on new material and keeping his act "authentic," but he has even gotten pretty darned good at horsemanship. His latest horse, Dusty, was trained entirely by Gary himself. Now, Dusty is not your ordinary run-of-the-mill horse either. In order to be in show business, Dusty has to be able to go indoors (or out), be around hundreds of people, and stay gentle enough that little kids and unsuspecting adults (who walk all around him and pet him from every angle) are safe when they do so.

Also, Dusty has to do something very unnatural for a horse: That is stand still in one spot, for long periods of time while this guy sits up there, strums the guitar, sings loudly, talks a lot, and moves around into different positions throughout the show. Dusty also knows show business tricks such as rearing up. Oh, and did I mention that Dusty has been doing all of this since he was only three?

Yes, Gary Sprague is quite a hand when it comes to getting his horses ready for entertainment. He says that he just shows them what he wants them to do and is gentle about doing it. (Sounds pretty simple, but have you ever tried it?)

Not only does Gary work hard at keeping his act authentic, but he also lives the lifestyle of a true cowboy. Sure he has attended brandings and worked cattle, logged thousands of hours in the saddle, trained his own horses, and looks like a cowboy, but, much more than that, he is a cowboy at heart. He is the kind of guy who is true to his word, always tries to do the right thing, lends a helping hand when he can, believes in God and country, and is one hundred percent true to his best friend and partner, his wife of thirty-seven years, Peggy.

Not only did he follow in the footsteps of the original pioneers and "Go west" in the middle of his life to experience a life change and become a true Westerner, but his beautiful Peggy has been right there

Gary preforms in many ways.   *Photo courtesy of Gary Sprague*

with him and supported and promoted him the whole way. If Gary's move from east to west, learning the trade of a cowboy and Western musician doesn't sound like a pioneer cowboy story from a hundred years ago, then I don't know what would.

Just like any true cowboy though, Gary is passionate about what he believes is right. For him, one of the ways to do that is by educating children. He loves to work with children, making several appearances each year to entertain and educate children at elementary and pre-schools. He has developed a special act, tailor-made, to help inform the youngsters about the cowboy way of life.

Gary also makes appearances to entertain the "old folks" who have no other way to get out and see something like his act. His visits to nursing homes are well-received by people there as it helps most of them go back to a time in their lives when people just like Gary were their heroes on screen.

He is especially proud of this work with both the young and the old, as it's kind of a "community service" he does. Yet, as he entertains tourists and corporate crowds, he's also proud of giving people a glimpse of an authentic cowboy from days gone by. He does as much to promote the image of the Old West to non-Western folks as anyone else out there. And he is respected for it.

Gary has his own special heroes. He always looked up to the heroes of the silver screen, but also has a deep respect for what he calls "the real cowboys" of the West. On one occasion, he entertained at world-champion team roper and past Professional Rodeo Cowboy Association president, Dale Smith's seventy-fifth birthday party. There were numerous world champion "gold buckles" in the crowd that night, as several past and present world champion cowboys were in attendance. Gary later said that he was in awe of some of the cowboys there, as a lot of those guys were heroes to him.

Gary had a lot of respect for the people in the crowd that night; yet, unbeknownst to him, the champion cowboys in the crowd were just as impressed by him as he was by them! They kept commenting about how neat it was that someone was carrying on the singing-cowboy tradition. The respect and admiration went both ways.

If you ever get the chance to see Gary Sprague, Arizona's Singing Cowboy, in action, you can expect to be entertained by that booming, charming voice, while he sings songs from a bygone era (and some more modern ones by request). He'll tell cowboy stories and recite poetry that will keep you laughing for hours. Gary is definitely a prime example of a real life cowboy hero.

Never become awed or afraid of the unknown. If Gary had listened to people back in New York telling him, "Moving to Arizona to become a western singer is nothing more than a pipe dream ..." he never would have succeeded!

Gary's normal work mode . Photo by Josh Ryan

Martin family photo

Don Martin

Hard Work Pays Off

On a beautiful August morning, a Southern Arizona cowboy decided to get in his twin-engine airplane and head north. His mission was to compete at the prestigious Arizona Cowpunchers Reunion and rodeo, an annual event held in the town of Williams. Shortly after arrival, the cowboy hops on a horse waiting for him there, then promptly wins the Calcutta and the Calcutta roping event. Total haul: $15,000 and trophy buckles. He then hops back in his plane, heading off into the wild blue yonder with a big smile, thinking back on a successful weekend.

This doesn't seem all that unusual to folks familiar with ropers and rodeo cowboys; that kind of thing takes place all the time throughout the West. What does make this your "not so ordinary" rodeo trip is that our hero is none other than an eighty-year-old Arizona native and cowboy who still flies his own plane and ropes good enough to "put a schoolin' " on younger generations.

This pilot/cowboy is Don Martin, born in Phoenix, Arizona, on January 23, 1926. As a youngster, one of Don's heroes was his uncle, Will Croft Barnes, who was a cowboy and a veteran of the Indian Wars of the late 1800s. Will Barnes was awarded the Congressional Medal of Honor for bravery during one of the battles with Indians.

Having a horse behind his house from an early age and listening to his uncle's stories and those told by his grandparents about the "olden days" inspired Don to want to be a cowboy when he grew up.

However, he enlisted in the Army when he got out of high school. That's where he was first introduced to flying, which became a lifelong enjoyment. After Don was discharged, he went to college to become a dentist, hopeful to earn enough money to buy a ranch someday.

After one semester, he thought, "If I have to spend several years smelling people's bad breath as a dentist just to earn enough money to buy a ranch, I don't want to do it. Maybe I'd rather just work in agriculture and *hope* to save up enough to buy a ranch instead." Don then changed his major to agriculture.

He competed on the college rodeo team as a bronc and bull rider. During the summers and between classes, Don worked at various cowboy jobs. Along the way, he came to the realization that, on a cowboy's wages, he would not likely save enough money to buy a ranch.

After college, Don went to work in feedlots for three different men over a period of eight years. Some of Don's early mentors were Levi Reed, Mo Best, and Olan Dryer. As Don worked for these men, they would allow him to run a few cattle of his own along with theirs. They did this out of appreciation for Don's willingness to work fourteen hours a day, seven days a week. Owning cattle supplemented his cowboy wages.

One day, Don and his partner of many years, Bill Brophy, found a feed yard for sale near Gila Bend, Arizona, they thought would be a good investment. The previous owners were willing to finance the two men. This purchase started a whole new chapter in Don Martin's life.

The partners operated Gila Feed Yard for twenty-eight years. They also ran cattle on a wide range of pastures, from New Mexico to California and from the Grand Canyon to the Mexican border.

In 1952, Don went on a blind date with Glenda Wold; the two have been together ever since. Don and Glenda have been happily married for about sixty years. Their four children are "good people," and their grandchildren are now making their marks in rodeo and ranching circles as well.

In the early years, Don and his family lived in Gila Bend. Later on, he moved his family back to Phoenix while he flew back and forth to the feed yard. Gila Feed Yard was a 30,000-head feedlot and was a successful operation until the two men decided to shut down the business in 1988. The success of Gila Feed Yard was attributed to the owners' honest and straightforward dealings mixed with a lot of fourteen-hour days.

After a while, Don was able to fulfill his dream of getting into the ranching business. In 1972, he bought the Rail X Ranch located near Catalina, north of Tucson. Today, the Martin family owns four different Arizona ranches: near Vail, Bonita, Elgin, and Catalina. They also own another ranch located near Roswell, New Mexico.

Don has always loved to rope; it's been a lifelong hobby of his. To this day, his children and grandchildren are all involved in roping and rodeos throughout Arizona and the Southwest.

Don Martin was one of the people who helped get the Arizona Junior Rodeo Association (AJRA) started and was its first president. He has also served on the Arizona Livestock Board and the Arizona Cattle Growers and the Arizona Cattle Feeders Associations boards. He has always enjoyed "getting involved" and "helping out" wherever he can. Being involved in those associations is just one of the ways.

Don says that, although his only regret in life was losing his oldest daughter, Becky, to cancer, he wouldn't go back and change a thing about his life. He says, "It couldn't possibly be any better the next time around."

At over eighty years of age, Don Martin still hasn't given any serious thought to retiring. He can still work fourteen-hour days with the best hands around, still flies his own airplane, and can still "get your money" at the ropings.

Those who don't believe "hard work pays off," need only to study the life of Don Martin for a contrasting point of view. Hard work and honest dealings contributed greatly to the success of this cowboy!

Jim Olson

Freed family photo

Steve Freed

The Beverly Hills Cowboy

In the race to find a cure for cancer, there are literally thousands of heroes. Many volunteer their time and money to further the cause. One man from the Southwest who stands out in this aspect is Steve Freed (aka "The Beverly Hills Cowboy") of Beverly Hills, California.

Steve was raised the son of a real estate entrepreneur. His first job was in a department store. He played tennis for Beverly Hills High School as a freshman. He was raised in an upscale neighborhood with Ernest Borgnine, Smokey Robinson, Debbie Reynolds, Shirley Jones, and Florence Henderson on the same block. Some may wonder, "How does a kid with a 90210 zip code grow up to be a cowboy?" But being a cowboy is exactly what Steve Freed wanted to do.

Steve was first introduced to horses at summer camp as a teenager. He loved being around the magnificent animals and longed to become a wrangler. He took to horses quickly and, in a short two-week period, was promoted to the position. It was his first paying job as a cowboy. He got to know another wrangler there who was a "real cowboy," and this guy took Steve to his first rodeo. There he became fascinated with the sport, telling his parents soon after, "I want to trade in my tennis racket and follow rodeo as a hobby instead." Needless to say, his parents were quite surprised.

Up to that point, Steve's main contact with the Western way of life had been through books and movies. Once submersed in the Western culture, Steve became an avid follower of men like Louis L'Amour,

John Wayne, and other "real cowboys" he chose to hang out with during his limited exposure to them in Southern California. This helped shape his moral code and the lifestyle he lives to this day.

Although Steve's road to becoming a cowboy was a bit "untraditional," today he represents the Western way of life as well as anybody. Steve is an avid team roper, a former saddle bronc rider, has been on ranch roundups, and even tried his hand at bull riding when younger. Oh yeah, did I mention he once road a wild buffalo!?

While an amateur rodeo contestant, he and a buddy went to watch a pro rodeo in Southern California one day to "see how the big boys do it." The contractor putting on the show asked Steve if he would ride a wild buffalo in the performance as a specialty act. Steve's friend warned him against tangling with the large, angry beast. Steve looked over the huge crowd and thought to himself, "This may be the only time I ever get to ride in a professional rodeo." So he told the contractor, "I'll do it." Unbeknownst to Steve, the guys who rode the buffalo before were now unable to due to injuries.

Steve competes at Team Roping.
Photo by Jennings Photography

While preparing for the ride, the rodeo announcer yelled down from the announcers stand, "Who is this guy, and where is he from?" He was informed it was Steve Freed from Beverly Hills. The announcer then proceeded to make a big deal about how no Beverly Hills cowboy was going to be able to ride a wild buffalo and had the crowd laughing in their seats with his jokes about it. Steve then felt he had something to prove.

When the chute flew open, 2,000 pounds of angry buffalo and Steve Freed made their way around the arena at a high rate of speed. The beast tried everything he had to lose his rider, but to no avail. When the ride was complete, Steve had won the respect of the announcer and the crowd. Thus the legend of The Beverly Hills Cowboy came about.

Fast-forward twenty years and Steve is a successful businessman and family man. He still longed for the thrill of cowboy competition, however, and still wanted to win his first belt buckle. In those years of competing on the rodeo circuit as a rough stock rider, he never won first place at a show giving out buckles. It now became a goal of his to win the coveted cowboy prize. As a testament of his stick-to-it-ness, Steve embarked upon a roping career, at forty years of age, excelling quickly.

At an age where most men are planning for a second home, a fancier automobile, and life to slow down a bit, he hit the team-roping circuit with unbridled passion. He won his first belt buckle as planned, even though he competed with a broken hand to do it. He was that determined! Steve, now an accomplished team roper, has numerous other prizes to his credit.

Aside from those superficial cowboy credentials, the most impressive thing about Steve is the code he lives by - "The Code of the West." Although Louie L'Amour and John Wayne may have been his heroes growing up, their fictional characters played a big role in molding Steve's own ethics and morals. Just like his heroes on the silver screen, with Steve, there is no "gray area." It is right or wrong - period. He even has a life-size cutout of "The Duke" in his office as a reminder of said code.

In true cowboy fashion, Steve is willing to lend a helping hand. His passion happens to be helping fund children's cancer research. Over the years, he has lent his time and money to literally help raise millions of dollars for the cause. From doing things, such as organizing a concert showcasing Stevie Wonder, Louie Anderson, and Quincy Jones, to traveling to Moscow to help facilitate an informational sharing program between the children's hospital there and Children's Hospital Los Angeles, Steve has been very involved in many aspects of the cause to find a cure.

Steve says, "I almost feel guilty because of the rewards I get from volunteering."

The year he turned fifty, friends and family were contemplating what kind of bash should be held in his honor. Steve started thinking about all the money they would spend on such a party and came up with another plan instead. It just so happened he knew of a doctor at Children's Hospital who was experimenting with some ground-breaking research to help relieve symptoms in children with brain tumors. The doctor needed $50,000 to kick off the project. Steve made it a goal to raise the needed capital.

In honor of his birthday year, Steve pledged to rope at as many team-roping competitions as he could get to and donate every dollar won. He counted on the rodeo community to get behind his cause as well in order to reach the fifty thousand. He says it was like celebrating his birthday all year long - much better, in his opinion, than a one-time, expensive birthday extravaganza.

At the end of the year, Steve did in fact present a check for $50,000 to Children's Hospital from The Beverly Hills Cowboy. Along the way, people heard about his cause, and he became somewhat of a legend in the rodeo world that year. Hundreds of folk pitched in to make Steve's goal come true. He made many new friends and gained much exposure for his cause along the way.

Steve says, "I may not be a scientist, and I can't sit in a lab. I don't have that educational background. But I can raise money for cancer research. I can help these researchers achieve their goals. They need funding; they can't find a cure without funding. That's how I am going to make a difference. That's where my passion for cancer research comes in."

Steve Freed is one of those great men who, not only keeps the West alive in an unlikely setting, but is also a great humanitarian. Men such as this make the world a better place to live.

Penrod family photo

Jack Penrod

Fun-loving Cowboy

One of Arizona's great old-time ropers passed away June 2, 2009. If you haven't heard of Jack Penrod or at least the Penrod name, you probably haven't attended many team ropings around the Southwest. Penrod's name has been synonymous with roping and rodeoing since the 1940s.

Eleven kids called Jack, "Dad." Thirty-three grandkids, cousins, and a multitude of relatives of Jack's keep up family traditions at some rodeo or roping every week. He had a huge impact on rodeo and ropings across the West in more ways than one. Roping was definitely his passion.

Jack was born, in 1932, on the family's homestead in Show Low, Arizona. Growing up during the Depression years, Jacks family had a small farming and livestock operation on the edge of Show Low (now it is inside the *city* of Show Low). But Jack wasn't interested in farming; all he was interested in back then was becoming a cowboy. As a young man, he got his uncle, Joe Stocks, a local top hand, to "show him the ropes" you might say. And become a cowboy is exactly what Jack did; he spent his entire life with the distinct title of "Cowboy!"

Not only did Jack become a cowboy, he became what you might call a "cowboy's cowboy." In his younger days, Jack was a top hand on any outfit where he chose to show up and he was a tough ol' booger to boot. Jack learned the cowboy trade in the rough mountainous country of Arizona, where most everything seems straight up and down. That high country is covered with tall pine trees, large pinion and juniper trees, and snow half the year. The lower country and canyon bottoms are strewn with large boulders and covered in cat claw or other sharp-edged plants. You *have* to learn to be a tough cowboy if you are going to survive a lifetime cowboy career in country like that. And survive a long and notable cowboy career is exactly what he did. Other than a brief stint as a meat cutter in a butcher shop and part-time logger/wood cutter, Jack was a cowboy his entire life. (The last few years of his life, he was also a restauranteur.)

Jack held several notable cowboy jobs throughout his lifetime, including being one of the "head stockmen" at the White Mountain Apache Reservation ranch for several years. Jack also had a feedlot in the deserts of Mesa, Arizona, where he traded cattle and horses, but he always preferred the high country. As he got older, he was a mentor to many young cowboys who respected his vast cowboy knowledge and abilities.

Jack loved to tell old cowboy stories as he got a few years on him, and one such notable story that only a high-country cowboy could associate with went something like this: Jack was working on the famous Bourdon Ranch northeast of Show Low during the late 1960s. In the winter of 1967 came the "great snow" - still talked about today by old-timers. Jack said it snowed so much only the rooftops of the houses could be seen in most places. Out on the ranch during the storm, they ran a dozer around trying to find live cattle and get feed to them. As little pockets of cattle were located, they fed them hay in the high-walled path left behind by the dozer. Before long, several hundred head of cattle were lined up in sort of a tunnel that had walls of snow higher than the dozer itself. Jack says they bladed the tunnel right out to a main road, where cattle trucks were waiting, and they loaded the cattle right into those trucks. No corrals were used. The snow banks were so high it was like the cattle were in an alley made of snow! They hauled the cattle to the desert where ephemeral feed was abundant, and everything turned out alright. Jack had hundreds of cowboying stories like that one, but his true cowboy passion in life was rodeo and jackpot roping.

In his younger years, Jack was a heck of a bronc rider, calf roper, and "tie down" team roper. Up until the 1970s, every little town around had its annual rodeo, parade, dance, celebration, and just general good time on a certain date. Jack went to all of them. These little rodeos and celebrations were a big deal to their towns, and they were just as big a deal to the cowboys, such as Penrod, who attended them each year. Cowboys would save up their wages all month, come to town on that special weekend, and "enter up" in hopes of winning the big prize. Jack won prize money and trophies all over. From southern Colorado and western New Mexico, to Arizona, Jack was a regular. Back then, when he showed up at the rodeo, everyone knew it was not going to be easy to beat him.

Like most rodeo cowboys seem to do, as Jack got older, he transitioned into being a team roper. After he got too old to compete and win consistently at the other events, Jack left bronc riding and calf roping to the younger generation. But right on up till the time he passed on, he competed regularly at jackpot team ropings!

Jack took roping very seriously and practiced it religiously. No matter what else he had going on, on certain days each week everything came to a halt at a predetermined time so Jack could practice. Being

Dallas Stock and Jack Penrod compete during the 1960s.
Photo courtesy of Penrod family

the tough ol' booger he was, it didn't matter much about the weather and such, 'cause he would keep right on roping. He'd say things like, "Well it might be like this at the roping, and we better practice for it." Just like in his younger years as a rodeo contestant, Jack was a regular at the pay window for jackpot team roping as well.

Another notable thing about Penrod was that he liked to have a good time. Now I know most everyone likes to have a "good time," but Jack went after a good time with lots of "gusto," just like he was entered in another competition. At the rodeo dances, Jack would dance until there was no one left to dance with or anyone left to play music! Jack loved dancing and having a good time so much that he was very popular with the ladies for his dancing abilities and his fun-loving attitude. Eight to eighty, blind, crippled, or crazy, Jack would dance with 'em all till they were give out. But there was one particular lady who could keep up with Jack and was the only one ever given credit for "taming" the wild and fun-loving cowboy.

Jack met Lucy Apodaca while working on the Table Top ranch near Stanfield, Arizona. Jack and Lucy hit it off immediately as they were both great dancers, and both had an endless energy for it. They would start off in the country dance halls and wind up in the Mexican dance halls before the night was over with. It didn't matter to the dancing couple, just keep playing music and they would keep right on dancing. Keep right on dancing is just what they did. Jack spent the last twenty-six years of his life with Lucy. She was the only one with the ability to keep Jack "in check" (albeit only somewhat).

As Jack got older, he took great delight in watching his kids at their own accomplishments, and his large family was a source of great pride to him, always putting a smile on his face when he spoke about them. Jack's far-reaching effect on roping can still be felt in arenas all across the West. Jack's relations and offspring compete each and every day, carrying on that great cowboy tradition that was so much a part of him.

Jack Penrod was definitely a "cowboy's cowboy." He was tough, a hard worker, and a top hand by anyone's standards. If you have seen movies or read books about cowboy characters, like those in *The Rounders* by *Max Evans*, for example – or if you have ever been fortunate enough to be around cowboys like that, then you know what Jack was like: a hard-working sure-enough "cowhand." But watch out when he came to town, because he liked to play and have a good time also.

It is a blessing to know someone with a good attitude toward life. It is even better if you possess such an attitude. Jack was liked far and wide, because he always had a smile on his face. His presence will forever be felt in arenas across the Southwest.

Jim Olson

Photo by "Betsy" courtesy of Honeycutt family

C.P. Honeycutt

Farmer to Hall of Famer

The community thought enough of him to name two roads after him in his hometown. He was the first Arizonan to be inducted into the National Cutting Horse Association (NCHA) Hall of Fame and the twelfth person overall. In a part of the world filled with big name, successful farmers, he stood as a giant among them. Family man, horseman, farmer, cattleman, civic-minded, friend, and neighbor - that was C.P. Honeycutt of Maricopa, Arizona.

When people conjure up images of cutting horses and cutting horse competitions, they think mostly in terms of Texas. Nearly all the people in the NCHA Hall of Fame are from Texas. C.P. Honeycutt was actually born near Athens, Texas, in 1909, but rose to fame as a cutter - from Arizona! What's even more amazing about the accomplishments of C.P. is he accomplished this, and so much more, only working at it part time. You see, he was a full-time farmer.

C.P Honeycutt came of age during what most of his generation only refer to as "the dirty '30s" (more commonly known as the Great Depression). Times were sure enough hard back then. C.P recalled later in life plowing endless hours with a team of mules, thankful just to have work. He'd tell stories of living in a crate on the side of the road, wondering where his next meal would come from. He never quite got over the feeling of being hungry, and it drove him to strive for great heights.

Things were so tough in Texas that, toward the end of the '30s, C.P., his wife, young daughter, brother, and sister-in-law decided to head west in search of a better life. They got as far as Eleven Mile Corner, Arizona, and pulled into a station there, almost out of gas. With less than one dollar between them, they were trying to decide whether to put more gas into the car and keep going west, or buy a loaf of bread and bologna so they could eat. A local farmer happened by the store right about then and, on a whim, C.P. approached him and asked if he needed any hands.

The man said the only job around at the time was picking cotton. He asked if they picked cotton. Now keep in mind, back in those days, cotton picking was done by hand and was hot, sweaty, backbreaking work. Well, ole C.P. proudly said he could pick more cotton than anybody, and he'd be willing to prove it!

Tom Carlton, impressed with C.P.'s spunk and determination, hired them on the spot. He told the man at the store to give Honeycutt all he needed, and, if they didn't come back and pay, he'd stand good for it. C.P. and his family did not disappoint.

After cotton harvest, Mr. Carlton decided he could not let a hard worker like C.P. go down the road, so he hired him full time. Fast-forward a couple of years: The two men were talking one day, and Carlton asked Honeycutt if he'd like to get started farming on his own. "Of course I would," was the reply, "but where would I get the money?" Tom Carlton knew a man like C.P. deserved a place of his own, knew he would make it if only given a chance, so he suggested that C.P go talk to a finance man he knew ... said he just might give him a start.

At the meeting with the finance man, C.P. laid out a plan of things he would need to get going. He was very conservative and tried to just ask for the bare minimum. When finished, the man asked if he was sure that was all he would need. C.P. assured him he could make it, if he only had the chance. To C.P.'s astonishment, the finance man agreed to every bit of it. As it turns out, Tom Carlton had arranged it beforehand and agreed to make the note good if C.P failed. C.P didn't find that part out till later.

From that humble beginning grew the Honeycutt farming enterprise, which at one point topped out at over 5,000 acres of cotton. Along with cotton, cattle, and grains, other crops were raised. Eventually the original farm near Eleven Mile Corner and another near Casa Grande was sold. The Honeycutt operation then relocated to Maricopa, Arizona. This was the early '50s, and C.P. was a standout farmer in a county full of great success stories from thereafter.

Once he had a little money put together, he branched out into cattle, as you would imagine any true Texan would. Of course, when you own cattle, you ought to own horses. Since his childhood days back in Texas, C.P. always had wanted to own great horseflesh. So, when he decided to start buying horses, he went for the best. He purchased three studs from the famous King Ranch of Texas and had them shipped by rail to Maricopa. That was the mid-1950s. The rest, as they say, is glorious history; he had discovered cutting horses.

Over the next 35 years, C.P. rode cutting horses every chance he had. He competed predominantly in Arizona, but also hit shows in California, Nevada, and Colorado. Once in a great while he was able to get away from farming duties long enough to make the long trip to Texas. But, it didn't matter where he competed; C.P. was a continual winner. Year after year would find him in the top ten in the nation, even though he never went at it full time. Matter of fact, he won so much in Arizona, California, Colorado, and Nevada part time, that he continually maintained a high ranking in national standings!

CP's induction into the "Hall of Fame."
Photo courtesy of Honeycutt family

Locally, C.P. was especially tough to beat. He won the Arizona cutting horse circuit more times than is easy to count and, at one point, was the champion three years running. C.P. was very involved in the Arizona Cutting Horse Association, serving as its president on different occasions. He also began bringing cutting competitions to area feedlots during the '70s and '80s. Fresh cattle during an event are always a must, and he came up with the idea that it's much easier to bring the competition to the cattle rather than truck cattle to competitions. It worked well for all involved.

C.P. was such an accomplished horseman that Hollywood contacted him to appear in a few different movies for horse-related scenes. This led to lifelong friendships with men like Lee Marvin, Roy Rogers, Gene Autry, James Arness, and other celebrities. Local newspapers often reported on the famous men coming to hunt birds at the Honeycutt farm. C.P was still riding his beloved cutting horses until about four months prior to his death at the age of eighty. Those horses gave him a life of enjoyment and great accomplishment.

C.P. Honeycutt raised a wonderful crop of kids and grandkids that were his pride and joy. He had two daughters, Pat and Judy, and a son, Charles. Sadly, his son was killed in a plane crash in 1976. Only in his late thirties, Charles's death was a tragedy to the family. C.P then became closer than ever to his remaining relatives. It has been said he was a great family man.

The Honeycutt farm happened to be just down the road from the Red River farm and feedlot owned by the famous partnership of Louis Johnson and John Wayne. C.P and Louie were good friends, as they were neighbors, and this, along with his other connections to actors, led to him becoming friends with Duke also. Later in life, the families of Honeycutt, Johnson, and Wayne often vacationed and hung out together, taking trips to see the sights.

The story of C.P. Honeycutt is an inspiring one, which shows us anyone, can succeed through hard work, perseverance, and living right. Not too bad for a poor cowboy who once lived on the side of the road in West Texas during the Depression!

Bill Clark

Tod Storey
My Best Friend

I once had a best friend, but then he died.
I think of him often - last night I cried.
There are great memories, hardships too.
He's in a better place now, this is true.

Tod N. Storey, born in Belen, New Mexico, 1969, was the most genuine person I ever met. Although not perfect by any stretch of the imagination, he was always himself and never put on to be anything more. That is just one of the reasons I liked him so much.

A funny little story between us involved the "N" of his middle name. It stood for Nestor with an "o" (an old Spanish name), but I used to call him Nester with an "e" (as in a cowboy's reference to squatters). Although I never actually saw his birth certificate, he swore his name was misspelled, and his father had actually put the "e" in there by mistake. Once I heard that, I usually referred to him as "Nester." I was the only one who got away with that, but it was all in good fun. He had a special name he called me also ... however I don't feel obliged to include it here. LOL! I didn't mind anyway - at least not from him. He was the only one who got away with that, but that's just how good friends are.

Tod was raised like a lot of New Mexico country kids: by parents who had ideals and morals dating back generations. Old-fashioned. He was raised hard and mean by his father and taught to love and respect by his mother. That's just the way things are. Growing up, he learned to hate one and love the other. But that too was normal for this type of parenting. Later in life he grew to love and respect them both. He knew each was trying their best in their own special way. Like most of us, he vowed to never make the same "mistakes" made on him. It is always easier said than done.

When Tod died in 1999, he had two young children: a boy who was three and a girl not quite two. They were the light of his life. Although he only had a three-year track record of parenting when he passed on, he was doing his darndest to raise his little ones to have the same morals and values he grew up with. He also wanted to keep their love and respect at the same time. Be friends with them. It is a fine line that many parents struggle with: How do you keep kids loving, and, more importantly *liking* you, while teaching them to be respectful, hard workers, polite, honest people, and with morals at the same time? My bet says he would have gotten it done. He was the best parent I ever saw. Tod loved kids and wanted to have a large family.

Actually, Tod loved people - and people loved Tod. If I had to say one thing that was his "claim to fame," something he was most noted for, it would have to be that most everyone liked him. He had the biggest heart of anyone I ever knew and more friends than anyone I have ever known. Tod's friends hung around with him, because they actually *liked* him, not because he had money to blow or other things to offer.

His friends were loyal. I believe that was because he had such a big heart - a heart bigger than the whole state of New Mexico. They say that "like attracts like," or that "you get what you give." I guess in that respect, I know why Tod had such a following of good and loyal friends.

Tod Storey may have been my best friend, but I am just about sure I am not the only one who would say that. While I have only had one "best friend" of that magnitude in my life, I honestly believe Tod had many. He touched people in that way. He made each and every person who was his friend feel they were important to him. And they were. He honestly cared about what his friends thought and how they felt. It wasn't just "chit chat" with him - he really cared. He was not the kind of person just trying to talk about what was going on in *his* life or what was important only to *him* at that moment. He wanted to know about you, *your* feelings and *your* life, because he cared about *you*. Not just you or I - but *all* his friends. He wasn't scared to make new friends either - that's how we met.

Tod worked for New Mexico Game and Fish Department. Photo courtesy of Storey family

Although both raised in New Mexico, we did not know each other until we were teenagers. We hit it off instantly. That was special to me. Finding someone with a similar upbringing, similar ideals, and experiences - someone I got along with so easily. That has only happened once in my life, but it was normal for Tod. As I said, he had hundreds of friends. In the years we were close friends, he touched my life in a very special and positive way.

With Tod, what you saw was what you got. He was an honest and open person. No hidden agenda. He often "wore his emotions on his sleeve," but he had nothing to hide. "If you stand upright and look a man in the eye, you've got no problems ... nothing to worry about," were words of his.

Being *genuine* like that is a quality hard to find in many. Tod was the kind of guy who could show up at a gathering somewhere, and, in a little while, he would have several new friends. People were attracted to him. Not only that, he would know details about people they normally would not share with a "stranger." After knowing Tod for just a little while, not many would claim he *was* a stranger. Folks would introduce him as "my new friend Tod ... with only one 'd.'" As I said, people just liked him.

Tod and son, Tanner. *Photo courtesy of Storey family*

No nonsense can also describe Tod. While he was a friend to so many, he also wouldn't put up with any "BS," if you know what I mean. If he did not like you or think you were a "good" person, he did not want anything to do with you. "To each his own," he would say. But if you crossed him or tried to push contrary ideals down his throat, you had better be prepared for a fight. I am reminded of the line in *The Shootist*, where John Wayne said something like, "I won't be wronged; I won't be insulted; and I won't be laid a hand on. I don't do these things to others, and I require the same from them." That was Tod to a "T." Don't mess with him, and he would leave you alone. But cross him, and you had better be prepared...

As a testament to his character, I offer this little story of a good time getting out of hand, but the right thing being done in the end: One night, about eight of us early twenty year-olds decided to make an appearance at a local cantina we often frequented. Being a bunch of poor rural kids, not many of us had vehicles that were very dependable, so that night, we hatched the bright idea to "ride a tractor to the bar!"

There was a little Ford tractor present Tod was using to do some maintenance around his place with a brush hog attached to the back and...this sounded like fun. We all could pile onto the hood, fenders, and brush hog...besides; we would also have the distinction of being the only ones there who drove in on a tractor.

Anyway, after a long night of good times, we headed back towards Tod's home, about six miles distant. We soon found out that with six of us on the brush hog in back, bouncing up and down, you could give a rider on the hood up front one heck of a ride...we made a sort of bronc/tractor riding contest out of it. The only drawback being the driver had little control over the tractor as the front tires only touched the ground periodically, spending most of its time in a "wheelie" fashion.

After several near-wrecks, our contest heated up to the point of getting out of hand and, as a result, tractor, brush hog and eight tipsy cowboys drove off the path we were on and through a farmers wire fence. The first thing we did was un-tangle the whole mess and get the tractor back onto the ditch bank again.

Immediately, it was obvious the fence had about twenty feet of major damage done to in. Several of the guys present wanted to leave the scene and vanish with nobody being the wiser. Tod was the first one to speak up and say, "There might be livestock loose in there - we have to find out." Over objections from a flighty few, he stood his ground and told them they could walk if so desired, but the tractor was not going anywhere till the situation could be assessed. I took up sides with him, but we were the minority.

Before long, a cautiously mad farmer came along shining a light. The first thing we asked was if there was any livestock in there and he said, "No." That being found out, Tod walked up to him, hand extended, and said, "My name is Tod Story and I will be back first thing in the morning to fix your fence, Sir." I admired the way he did that, by giving his name, he couldn't shirk the duties of fixing the fence without public shame. Inspired to do right, I stepped forward and did the same. A few of the guys chastised us and said we were crazy, that old farmer never would have known who did it. Tod simply said, "I would know."

The next morning at six, Tod rousted me out of bed and said, "Let's go fix fence," and we did. When we were almost done with the job, the farmer came out and said, "I didn't think you guys would return," and with a hint of piety added, "Most drunks wouldn't have."

The remark stung deeply and as we went about our merry way, I wanted to be mad about our reception from the old timer. Tod calmly told me, "Let him think what he wants. Just because we drink and have a good time does not make us bad people. We don't have to act like low-lifes just cause some think we are. If we would have run off like so-and-so wanted to do last night, then that old man would have been justified in his thinking about us. I personally would not give him the satisfaction. I know in my heart that his fence is in better shape now than when we drove into it last night. How he chooses to look at it is his problem."

Tod had bad scars on his body from being in several unnecessary car wrecks. Normally it was this type of situation: He'd have relationship problems; numb the mind; then drive off hurt in a mad rage. That, my friends, is a deadly combination. However, he was only human and fought the same demons most do when dealing with life's situations. It just about got him a couple of times - a couple of times he escaped the Grim Reaper when he probably shouldn't have - but it finally caught up with him. Nobody dances with death for long without paying the price.

On October 15, 1999, one month to the day after his thirtieth birthday and distraught from divorce proceedings going on in his life, Tod died in a single-vehicle accident. Some say it was booze; some say it was other things; some even had the audacity to blame personal situations. But I know no one forced him into the truck on that fateful day, he was in control of his own actions and nobody else was hurt in the deal.

I had a very long visit with him on his thirtieth birthday that month before. We talked of many things, laughed, shared sadness and discussed philosophy. Looking back on it now, I know in my heart, it was just his time to go. I believe it was God's way of bringing him home... there are bigger things at work that we have no inkling of during this mortality.

Tod Storey was one of the greatest human beings I have ever come into contact with. He made me want to do better just by being around him. Even in our younger, wilder days, when most would not have given us a snowballs chance in the desert of making anything of ourselves, he still held his head high.

It's been some years now since he passed on, but his presence is felt in my heart and in the hearts of many others to this day. Tod left a big footprint in a short time. He lived more life in thirty years than some people live in a lifetime lasting two or three times as long. We used to talk about living each day like it might be your last, and that is exactly how he did it. No regrets, no stone left unturned, and no adventure left undone. That's commendable!

After more than a decade, I look back on the memories and experiences with a gleam in my eye. We danged sure had a lot of fun. Yet, on the other hand ... it still hurts. I am just proud to have been blessed to share the time I was given with such a great human being. My friend ... I miss you.

I conclude with the story of Tod Storey because he was an inspiration to me. Although he never aspired to be anything out of the ordinary, his was a spirit of naturally high standards. Definitely not a perfect person, but for sure "personably perfect."

About the Author

Western Writers of America member

Jim Olson is a ranch-raised cowboy, author, promoter and entrepreneur. He grew up on the high plains of eastern New Mexico, learning to ride young colts, tend to cattle and drive heavy farm equipment at an early age.

Jim spent some years competing in the calf roping event at the Professional Rodeo Cowboys Association level, qualifying for the circuit finals a few times. Now he is a weekend roper. He lives on and operates his own ranch near Stanfield, Arizona - once a part of John Wayne's Red River Ranch.

These great life experiences Jim now uses in his writing career. He writes stories about interesting and extraordinary people of the west including short stories of both fiction and nonfiction. He writes a monthly column titled "My Cowboy Heroes," published by several Southwestern and national magazines. Jim has three published books and can be reached through his website at www.jimolsonauthor.com

CPSIA information can be obtained at www.ICGtesting.com
Printed in the USA
BVOW041653280213

314358BV00001B/3/P